CELEBRATION AND
EXPERIENCE
IN PREACHING

More praise for
Celebration and Experience in Preaching,
REVISED EDITION:

"Reading this revised edition of *Celebration and Experience in Preaching* feels like sitting with a wise sage whose deep faith can barely be contained on the page. Henry Mitchell is above all a faithful preacher. In this book he is also a teacher, giving us clear guidelines for preaching that take emotion as seriously as intellect. Those who have read the original book will find much here that is new, especially clear charts that show how a sermon moves. If you missed the original, you'll be grateful you didn't miss this one."

—Barbara K. Lundblad,
    Joe R. Engle Professor of Preaching,
    Union Theological Seminary

Celebration
and
Experience
in
Preaching

REVISED EDITION

Henry H. Mitchell

ABINGDON PRESS
NASHVILLE

CELEBRATION AND EXPERIENCE IN PREACHING
REVISED EDITION

Copyright © 1990, 2008 by Abingdon Press

This book is printed on acid-free paper.

Library of Congress Cataloging-in-Publication Data

Mitchell, Henry H.
  Celebration and experience in preaching / Henry H. Mitchell.—Rev. ed.
    p. cm.
  Includes bibliographical references and index.
  ISBN 978-0-687-64919-8 (pbk. : alk. paper)
  1. Preaching. I. Title.

  BV4211.3.M58 2008
  251--dc22

                                                                    2008027057

08 09 10 11 12 13 14 15 16 17—10 9 8 7 6 5 4 3 2 1

MANUFACTURED IN THE UNITED STATES OF AMERICA

CONTENTS

ACKNOWLEDGMENTS AND PREFACE TO THE REVISED EDITION

The first edition of *Celebration and Experience in Preaching* was published in 1991. Since then, it has been quoted in the works of other homileticians. However, they and I, too, have learned much more about preaching in the intervening years, and we have learned better ways to communicate what we already knew. Some of the basic ideas in *Celebration* have ceased to need prominent placement here, because they tend now to be taken for granted. Nevertheless, some folk may still require the supporting understandings of human consciousness put forth in the first edition; this material has been relocated to the Appendix. And, of course, much of the first edition needs updating, restating, and reorganization.

Two aspects of this work which seem still to want for clarity in the popular mind are Black preaching's inescapable rootage in two main cultures, and this work's wider interpretation of that rootage as intended for *all* cultures. The strengths of the African American pulpit tradition have never been God's gift for "Black people only." Just as Euro-American pulpit tradition has been taught as valid for all people, so also has the best of the Black pulpit tradition been willingly shared. It needs to be just as well received among other cultures and their pulpits.

The decline of "mainline" congregations, denominations, and pulpits especially, has already moved many White seminaries quietly to seek inevitably bicultural African American teachers of homiletics. Popular television ministries of Whites have also already appropriated the riches of the best of the Black tradition. It is high time *all branches of American Christendom* chose and confessed to a single, integrated, comprehensive corpus of the best of everybody's preaching wisdom, as drawn from whosoever has the gifts. It was in this frame of mind that this book was first written, and is still written.

Essential to this ideal of a comprehensive corpus of preaching wisdom is a shared vocabulary—an emergent common terminology. Such a language is possible if and when scholars seek to understand and use one another's widely identified and accepted contributions, no longer needing attribution. I trust I may be understood when I suggest that the term *celebration* is such a term. To associate my race or name whenever this word is used is to imply an ethnic sole ownership, which is not desired, nor should it be felt required for professional academic credit. After so long a time, to accept and honor a term is to refuse to stop short of including that term in one's own working vocabulary. I must engage in this same kind of unmarked inclusion of many terms contributed by others, but long in common use. The term "move in consciousness," originally introduced by David Buttrick, has likewise evolved into common use, requiring, as I see it, no further attribution.

Much that I could have wanted to say has been better said *for* me by James A. Forbes Jr., in the foreword to the first edition. In deep gratitude to him, I have sought and been given permission to include that foreword in this revised edition.

Profound thanks are also still due to the classes taught and the audiences who have listened and reacted to lectures given. To these must now be added the homileticians who have honored and reacted, in their own books and lectures, to my work. Without these interactions the progress hopefully made since the first edition would not have been possible.

Finally, all praise and thanks are due to God, in obedience to whom all my work is attempted, and whose inspiration and guidance are crucial to what, if anything, I have contributed. Ordinarily, one doesn't insert footnotes saying, "God gave this to me." Yet, in a very real sense, every fresh insight from my pen is a personal gift from the God of all truth, all authentic scholarship, and all human communication, to whom I most humbly and willingly assign any and all credit and praise.

Henry H. Mitchell, 2008

FOREWORD

TO THE FIRST EDITION

What Henry Mitchell writes about preaching has been tested on the road for more than a half a century and refined in the classroom for half that time. The wisdom and insights he shares have been exposed to loving critique by scores of his students, ministerial colleagues, and teachers of preaching. In addition to his professorial responsibilities, he has been at the center of an informal dialogue on preaching with friends and acquaintances from a wide cross section of denominations and regions of the country.

I have enjoyed membership in both the formal and informal sections of Mitchell's academy of homiletics. His *Black Preaching* (Harper & Row, 1979) helped me affirm with pride gifts I had inherited from a vibrant African American homiletical tradition. His mentoring in the Martin Luther King Jr. Black Church Studies Program at Colgate Rochester Divinity School deepened my understanding of the unique contribution Black preaching could make for the empowerment of the broader ministry of the Word.

As a professor of homiletics in a predominantly White seminary, I found that Mitchell's *Recovery of Preaching* provided an invaluable enrichment of perspective when used with the bibliography of the guild. His work has a way of identifying issues largely neglected by others in the field, or at least of making much clearer those issues they often fail to emphasize.

Drawing upon his earlier volumes, Mitchell picks up the theme of celebration and "movements in consciousness," and expands upon the why and the how of these elements in the preaching task. He gives specific instructions on how to move from lackluster communication to superlative proclamation, which gets the hearers "on board" in the dynamic of the biblical story. He shows how a commitment to engaging the whole person—spirit, intuitive mind, and emotive consciousness—increases the prospect that the preaching event will be a transformative experience.

Whereas Mitchell's earlier works emphasized the Black church tradition almost exclusively as his primary source, this book [original edition] acknowledges that the evangelical preaching tradition, shared by

Blacks as well as Whites, has drawn from various streams to perfect a broad preaching profile. Thus one will experience this effort as a bridge across the ethnic abyss, bringing fresh strength to all who engage in the exchange. This work will break open new possibilities for those who have viewed preaching for so long as primarily rationalistic enterprise. At the same time, it will share with the opposite group a set of terms and disciplines with which to refine and focus the marvelous powers of a folk tradition.

Finally, let's give Henry Mitchell, the dean of imaging and the hearers' identification, his due. We are the recipients of his more than fifty years' labor of love to tell us what the great preachers of time all along have been saying by way of their sermons: "The people" need a picture from God to take with them on their journey; "the people" need to hear from your mouth that you have translated with your head the issues that flow through the heart of humanity. Without minimizing the crucial significance of the cognitive dimension, Mitchell effectively questions the adequacy of theories and practices of proclamation that bows down at the altar of the Enlightenment, passing over the Puritan piety of heartfelt religion. Mitchell not only calls for a proper balance of head, heart, and hands; he shows us how to do it. The cure for the "common coldness" that attends too much preaching has been available in our lifetime. Our thanks to God the giver, and to Henry Mitchell the distributor. I expect many preachers to discover in the pages that follow the clue to a quality of delivery that will turn the experience into a very powerful occasion of celebration.

James A. Forbes Jr., March 9, 1990

PART I

THE EXPERIENCE OF THE WORD

It is my deep conviction that the salvation of the soul and its spiritual growth come through a spiritual experience, and that preaching at its best is used by the Spirit to bring an *experiential* encounter with the Word. This is not the same thing as sincere intellectual assent to a reasonable system of belief as primary in the Christian's life, nor is it a formal statement of faith. These come *after* the experience of faith, to describe, interpret, and help communicate that experience, rather than to validate it.

To be sure, there must be words to express one's faith, and they must make sense. Our deep belief must fit together cogently in the statements with which we witness to our faith. If not, the hearer's reason will screen the witness out as nonsense. However, although faith is not based on logic and cogency, logical arguments can well be used to disprove and remove intellectual obstacles to faith in the minds of sincere seekers. For instance, a logical argument must be used against the false assumption that the human mind can comprehend all things, leaving no room for faith. At this point, reason plays a very important role, but it doesn't *generate* faith; reason just supports faith after the fact.

The human intuitions and emotions of trust aren't hard data; they are the gift of the Spirit, through the *experience* of the whole person. The Apostle Paul soundly declared that "hope" that is visible leaves no rational necessity for hoping (Rom. 8:24). Faith, hope, and love are emotions and intuitions, and they are given to us through experiences of the Spirit, for which we can take no works-type credit. We are saved by faith, which very definitely is not a work, not even a work of the mind. Sermons can't argue people into faith or trust. All the preacher can do is, with the help of God, design and deliver an experience of God and the Word, or "make straight the highway" for our God the Holy Spirit to convey the gifts of saving faith and growth. The three chapters that follow are all focused on assisting the preacher to understand and prepare for this task.

After devotional discipline, that preparation toward meaningful experiential encounters with the Word can best be carried out by assuring that three major elements are present: (1) a text from the Bible, encouraging trust in and obedience to the Word, together with a behavioral purpose that flows from that text, enabling clear focus on the application of the text to real life; (2) an understanding of experiential encounter, enabling identification with and into the Word; (3) an understanding of emotion, the timing of suspense, and the role of climactic celebration, enabling ecstatic reinforcement of the text and its behavioral purpose (b.p.). These three elements are described in part I, chapters 1, 2, and 3.

Part II describes the language and image vehicles necessary for the design of meaningful experiences. Part III deals with mechanical concerns, such as opening a sermon, and with concerns regarding the place of the Spirit in such detailed sermon preparations as are recommended here.

CHAPTER 1

The Definition and Purpose of Experiences of the Word

Actually, God gives experiential encounters in the Spirit and with the Word. Yet, quite often, these experiences occur in apparent connection with the efforts of thoughtful servants of God. It is a fact that we are commanded to go into all the earth and preach and teach and witness as if it all depended on us, while trusting that it all is in the hands of God. For the homiletical studies outlined in this work, then, preaching is defined as follows:

To preach is so to be used by the Holy Spirit that the gospel is communicated, to the end that hearers are saved and then helped to grow in grace and in the knowledge of our Lord. It is the hope of every preacher that every sermon will be used by the Spirit to move Christians to grow from point A to point B, in the direction of the life modeled by Jesus Christ. And every sermon should focus on one such behavioral goal as stated or implied by the biblical text.

The first element of meaningful experiential encounter is a *biblical text*, the basis of the authority that distinguishes the sermon from a secular essay. Texts should be chosen with careful thought, as well as divine guidance. In the thoughtful aspect, a text should be chosen for clarity of *behavioral purpose* and memorable brevity, as well as for helpful guidance in a specific human need. Some texts literally *are* behavioral purposes: "In every thing give thanks" (1 Thess. 5:18). Other texts imply or exemplify behavioral purposes (b.p.). In Romans 8:28, Paul exemplifies a b.p. of trust in all situations when he says, "We *know* that God works in everything for good (author's translation; emphasis mine)." Because so many texts imply trust, this b.p. should be more specific: "Regardless of fearful appearances, God works in *everything!*"

Jesus' Parables have implied b.p.s. For instance, there is no direct admonition to "be compassionate," but the parable of the good Samaritan (Luke 10:33) says it all in a human example of compassion. This one-purpose focus is characteristic of all of Jesus' parables, and Matthew, Mark, and Luke all testify that this is how Jesus preached

(Matt. 13:34; Mark 4:34; Luke 8:10). He employed concrete images that had parallels to spiritual meanings, otherwise expressible only in abstraction.

To attempt more than one purpose is likely to achieve neither or none, because of lack of focus. It is a great and sufficient blessing when the gospel concerning even one needed behavior is actually received and the hearer is motivated and empowered to obey. For example, "Blessed are the meek" (Matt. 5:5) is a great challenge. One hardly dares ask the Spirit for more in a single sermon. (Notice, Jesus didn't say, "You *ought* to be meek.")

One is not necessarily called to preach all of even one text verse if it contains more than one behavioral goal. Paul's great list of the fruits of the Spirit includes seven goals in Galatians 5:22, with two more in verse 23. I have been known to preach for two weeks, with introductory and concluding sermons and a different fruit from the text for a b.p. each night of a ten-night revival.

These guidelines of brevity and clarity are often challenged in class on the grounds that all of a verse ought to be treated. A long, Paul-type sentence (Ephesians 3:15-19 is just one sentence) offers many possible b.p.s. Students feel obligated to preach all of them, exhausting all possible meanings. Of course, even for one brief verse, this just simply may be impossible. But the most important response to the challenge to exhaust meaning is that the goal of one sermon is *not* comprehensive knowledge of so little as one whole verse; it is the faithful change of life in the direction of no more than one Christlike characteristic, as called for in the Word.

As stated before, there is a need to avoid confusing mental agreement or affirmation with living, obedient faith. In this vein of thought, students often submit sermon texts that seem to suggest as their b.p. a goal using verbs like "to know" or "to show." They want the hearer to "know" that God is provident—and this is good as far as it goes. Every b.p. requires some form of idea knowledge, but the bottom line is not just "knowing" and reciting a text. The bottom-line b.p. is trusting and obeying that text. One may agree that God is provident (Rom. 8:28), but the real test is whether or not the hearer can be calm and *trust* God's providence in times of hard trial. So to speak, this is a behavior at "gut level," a holistic confidence. About doctrines like God's providence, sermons on trust texts seek not so much theological knowledge as spiritual power that radiates from print and pulpit, out of the idea stage and into gut-level trusting under stress.

No less misleading than "to know" is the students' submitted b.p. "to show." The preacher, not the hearer, does the showing. It assumes intellectual processes and seeks agreement. Showing is what a lawyer does to convince a jury, from whom to win a decision. With a similar b.p., the *preacher* would be "showing" in a sermon while the audience or jury in the pew would listen passively and be expected to do no more "behavior" than a yes or no. The world needs good lawyers "to show," but not in the pulpit. Preaching is art, not argument. Spiritual encounters are not legislated or decreed; they are *experienced*.

THE LESSON AND LECTIONS IN WORSHIP

The usual Scripture lesson read in public worship is the one from which the text and b.p. have been drawn. However, there are occasional exceptions. These come from a text containing a well-stated b.p., but without supportive material in its biblical context. Such is the case with Romans 8:28, Paul's classic word about the providence of God. As will be stated in chapter 9, such a text may call for a lesson to be read from a different pericope that embodies this same b.p. In this case, Romans 8:28 calls for Genesis 50:14-21 as a lesson, with emphasis on verse 20, used in the sermon's celebration: "God meant it for good" (NKJV). This is not proof-texting; it is enriching an encounter by means of powerfully illustrating a similar and otherwise contextually isolated text about providence.

A widely utilized factor in the choice of sermon texts and lessons is the *Revised Common Lectionary*, offering preaching lections for a three-year cycle, including every week a reading from the Hebrew Bible, a psalm, an epistle, and a reading from the Gospels. Although some consider this restrictive, others, including whole denominations, see it as a safeguard against a temptation to stay on one theme and to overemphasize one part of the Bible. In any case, lectionaries have passages from all four parts of the Bible, each of which has verses from which the Spirit may guide a text to be found that fits a congregation's needs, and a given preacher's gifts and passionate convictions.

For those who resist the lectionary itself, lectionary-type options include the individual's own design of a year's preaching plan or a series of sermons on the life of Christ, the great prophets of the Old Testament, or exciting characters like David and Deborah, Priscilla and Paul. The main concern is to preach from a whole Bible in all its aspects, reaching the whole gamut of human need. This requires some form of

Spirit-guided discipline with some continuity of flow and direction. Such planning seeks to equip members for the abundant life of faith and service, and avoids the virtual certainty of falling into a rut where one's texts are selected from too typical, week-to-week options presumably offered by the Spirit.

POSITIVE FOCUS

All of this concern for disciplined singleness of b.p. can be called *focus*. It is used to maintain audience attention, with the draw made possible by flow in one direction, for one positive purpose. Careful focus on text and b.p. has the literary purpose of keeping hearers aboard a single experience until it has landed. Every part of the sermon is subject to the test of whether it contributes to the experiential encounter with the text and inspires the acceptance of and trusting obedience to the text and b.p.

It should be noted, however, that all passages of Scripture are not amenable to use as sermonic texts. An extreme example of this is seen in the fact that no preacher would dare take Psalm 137:9 (or Isa.16:13) as a text. It predicts: "Happy shall he be, that taketh and dasheth thy little ones against the stones." Many passages are potentially useful in context, including Psalm 137:9, but the main text should be a brief, memorable, positive guide for life, not a "what not to do." Indeed, the entire gospel is good news. Some may manipulate congregations with fear by using negative news, but perfect love casts out such fear (1 John 4:18).

When a negative text is the only one available for a worthy purpose, the positive counterpart of that purpose needs to be given twice as much emphasis or space. Jesus warned about the spiritual vacuum created by predominant negatives in the parable of the empty house (Matt. 12:43-45). His b.p. was, "Fill your house full with good things and leave no space for evil." In warning against negatives he created a positive, but this was a rare exception to the general rule against negative texts for main focus, and against sermons with more than a third of the space devoted to criticisms and vivid images of evil.

It should be understood that all this advice about choosing the b.p. is not born of an excessive ambition to gain full control of the results of the encounters discussed here. All of these results are still in the hands of God, but God does commission us (Matt. 28:19-20) to use our most thoughtful efforts to teach and preach. This emphasis on focus and b.p. is to help people stay gladly focused; because they will know they won't have to endure the too-common scene where the preacher "mounts his horse and rides off in all directions."

One other caution regarding the maintenance of focus deals with the temptation to insert irrelevant "pearls." The pastor or student has worked long and hard in research for the sermon, and has come up with some real jewels. When advised to delete some of these gifts from God as irrelevant, the student objects: "God must have wanted these jewels in this sermon, since they were given during preparation for this sermon. These jewels are also much too good to be wasted."

The answer to this challenge is simple: "Don't waste it; just don't use it here." It is good to keep on reserve a treasure trove or handy file of good ideas (God-given and otherwise) for those Fridays when the Spirit hasn't said a word all week and there is need for an inspired word for Sunday. You'll be glad you saved the jewels you couldn't use when received, and that you kept the original sermon focused on its text and b.p.

In reference to those moments of inspiration when ideas just pour in, it is wise to follow two rules. One is to capture the flow. Record all of it as it floods in, regardless of whether it fits for Sunday or not. Don't edit it for spelling, grammar, or anything else. Just record it while it is "hot," and before you let it slip into oblivion.

Rule two is later to sort through the flow, placing the items for immediate use in the flow of the tentative outline. Make sure the leftovers are legible and place them in a file that is organized by the books of the Bible, placing the jewels with whatever text they seem to fit. Another basis for organization of ideas may be a file of vital topics or burning contemporary issues. I am one of many preachers who testify that some of their best sermons were written under sudden emergency circumstances and using material from this file. This should be heard as advice that every preacher should have such an overflow file of material personally considered relevant and known to draw attention. Nevertheless, the blessing of the unprepared but effective use of such a file should be anticipated only in authentic, dire emergencies.

THE LIMITS OF RESPONSIBILITY

A final concern within this discussion of behavior is the fear of some that so much emphasis on human behavior seems to border on salvation by works. Shouldn't there be goals and purposes such as education about the Bible and the doctrines of the church? Shouldn't the pastor just do a teaching sermon from time to time? The answer is that *all* sermons should teach, but no sermon should be about history, geography, or doctrine that has no clear implications about behavior. Lessons of history and maps of Paul's journeys can be interesting and enlightening in classes, but not in a sermon, except as setting. The gospel was made for salvation and spiritual growth, not to create experts on Palestine. However, expert data from training-class sources can be used as details in sermons to make them come alive as encounter.

Meanwhile, whenever persons are saved and helped to live by faith, we will know it by their behavior and works (James 2:18). To preach the words of faith and not be used to move hearers to the works of that faith would be an exercise in futility.

Furthermore, it should be understood that focus on the b.p. is used to hold the sermon together as a work of art. Just as dramas and symphonies have a central theme throughout, so a sermon needs a center for artistic and attention-keeping reasons. Thus the b.p. is at the very heart of both the Bible text from which it comes and the artistry that brings to life the experiential encounter with the Word.

We move now from emphasis on the text and its behavioral purpose to emphasis on the encounter with the Word as experienced by the hearer.

CHAPTER 2

The Experience of Seeing, Hearing, and Believing

The second of the three elements necessary to experiential encounter of the Word is a basic understanding of the hearing and other senses and how they relate to belief. All human experience is first perceived via the five senses, whether physical data or human emotion. One can't get angry or glad about a thing until one sees and hears what it is. The mind *senses* what is happening in a human context by means of reports from the eyes, ears, nose, tongue, and touch. Every experience is in interaction with a specific person, place, or thing. Abstract ideas may flit through the rational mind, but the well-remembered *experience* of the whole person (body, mind, and spirit) begins always with sense-reported data.

Human experience is not recalled in words and sentences in print; memory is in images or pictures. Although a story or account may come to us in words, the image formed in our recall of the story will be in "color TV," so to speak. If a preacher wishes to be used of the Spirit to lead hearers into an experience of the Word, that preacher must provide clear word pictures or images for that experience.

Many years ago I heard C. A. W. Clark preach on David and Goliath. Clark's portrayal of both characters was so vivid that I could visualize their brief battle as from an excellent seat in the stands beside the battlefield. This vividness was not by chance. The preacher had given me the sort of details that are published in expensive football programs: Goliath's exact height and the length of his spear. Now, years after that revival, I can describe David's slingshot from easy memory. I was so caught up in the sermon that I had no spare attention for notes, and no need. With my privileged seat, who could forget such a great victory for the underdog? I'm short of stature compared to Goliath. David's victory was mine too because I identified with him!

The components of this description of a hearing experience are the subjects of this chapter. They are: (1) vivid details and images;

(2) familiarity, identification, and vicarious experience; (3) homiletic moves in consciousness. God uses these simple ingredients to enable the message to reach and influence the souls of whole congregations.

VIVID DETAILS AND IMAGES

As we have already seen, Matthew, Mark, and Luke all reported that Jesus always preached in parables. Each had a behavioral purpose, and every last one of them was done in images or word pictures. We often wish the Bible text had gone into greater detail, but we understand how hard it was to write all those details with a quill pen dipped in ink (no ballpoint pens or fountain pens). Jesus probably described more than the author was able to write, or the writer may have just known that we would fill in the details with our own familiarity with the subject. In any case, we know that Jesus said more than is in the Bible's precise but very brief wording. Thus, the preacher has to study hard and pray for the kinds of authentic, historical, fill-in details that make a person, place, thing, or a whole story come to life in the mental processes and total experience of the hearer.

The details needed come from several exegetical readings of the biblical material, plus consulting other resources. Preaching in images is not easy; it is at least as demanding as preparation for the traditional cognitive emphasis. As one reads, one screens for sensory data such as color, size, texture, shape, sound, temperature, distance, smell, and taste. Even age is a kind of visible data, although often inaccurate. Emotional data are very important; these are treated in chapter 3.

Detailed images in stories and all other genre are a nonnegotiable requirement for experiential encounter. They always were, and they always will be. In a 2004 interview with Oprah Winfrey, Barack Obama put it this way: "Images, actions, and stories always speak the loudest. . . . Policy has to be guided by facts, but to move people you have to tell stories."[1]

Some of the most effective details are right in the biblical text. For instance, when Jesus wanted to portray the desperation of the prodigal son, he noted that the young man was so hungry he "would fain have filled his belly with the husks that the swine did eat: and no man gave unto him" (Luke 15:16). In California's San Joaquin Valley, in a sermon on this parable, I happened to translate husks into the word used on the local farms where hogs were raised: *slop*. The response was awesome; the parable and the entire sermon took on a whole new life in the realism of the response of the farmers' own stomachs. The scene of the pig sty became their very own farmyards, and the crowning detail of odor was all too familiar.

Most of the effective details aren't this easy to find. They have to be located in study and extended realistically. Just as a realistic report of a lynching is too horrible to bear, so also is a report on the Crucifixion. Yet the preacher owes it to the hearers to describe how the cross was made, how Jesus was nailed onto it on the ground, and how it was stood up in a post-hole. This is not the polished cross on a church steeple; we need to see all of its gory dimensions in order to sense the suffering of our Lord, as well as the awesomeness of human cruelty and sin.

Here was a crude cross, hewed out with an ax, with burrs left sticking out because the pole hadn't been planed at a mill. This cross was laid on the ground and Jesus was laid on it, burrs and all. The ground held the cross firm as the nails were driven into Jesus' flesh. A post-hole had been dug, and then the cross was tilted up and dropped into the post-hole. It hit the bottom of the hole with a thud, and all of Jesus' body weight was suddenly pulled against the nails and the burrs. No wonder the tough centurion, who could defeat each of his hundred men in hand-to-hand combat, wasn't tough enough to take what he saw Jesus endure in silence! His exclamation could have cost him his top-sergeant stripes, but what did it matter? "Truly this man was the Son of God" (Mark 15:39). Details like these are loaded with vividness and well worth the work it takes to find them and make the picture come alive.

FAMILIARITY, IDENTIFICATION, AND VICARIOUS EXPERIENCE

The powerful impact of the key images and details portrayed thus far is because of their familiarity and the close associations many of the hearers may have. In churches where I preach often, I am one of untold numbers who have done construction labor. For us the mere mention of a post-hole brings up vivid details for the image of the Crucifixion as a whole. (I once got seven blisters from digging 110 postholes on my job!) With this bridge, our *association* with hard labor attaches us to the whole account and helps us *identify into it experientially*.

Another string of associations comes into play likewise, with military veterans and their families, when the centurion's rank is translated to "top sergeant" and the possible loss of his "stripes" is mentioned. From another angle, I heard a retired college president describe the leather garments of Roman soldiers and relate the fact that the soldiers all smelled bad because their "leathern" girdles could not be sent to a laundry. The high-school campers in the audience were then able not only to see and hear the tough centurion; they could smell him as well. They could associate him with basketball players in the locker room. All of these familiar details, with which the hearer has associated memories, add to the vividness and to the hearers' identification into the experience of the Word.

Details are essential to the impact because they enlarge depth of *meaning*. One of Jesus' most cleverly meaningful parables was about the wheat and the tares. Jesus' b.p. was to move hearers to avoid the irresponsible way they judged one another. I felt compelled to preach it after we planted the new parsonage lawn. An amazing problem arose when we found that for the first few weeks or so *all* the plants coming up looked just alike—grass and puncture weeds included. Both looked equally innocent. Yet eight weeks later those same plants would puncture a new bike tire riding across the yard. If we had tried to sort them out and pulled up the puncture weeds while both were still tender we would have wasted half of the new lawn by pulling up tender grass as well. In that neighborhood full of puncture weeds, the parable virtually preached itself on a realistic subject of known sensitivity concerning small-town, judgmental gossip.

All of this familiar association and identification leads to *vicarious experiences*—copies of experiences that can serve in place of the originals. That is to say, we learn the lesson and hopefully make the behavioral commitment as if we had lived through the biblical passage in our own flesh. The preachers study the lesson so thoroughly that they feel like eyewitnesses. In turn, they tell it so well that the hearers feel as if they were there too, witnessing with their own ears and eyes. This leads to commitment to the behavioral purpose (more about this later). For instance, when hearers identify with Paul in his text about being content in whatsoever state (Phil. 4:11), they will seek to share that same contentment in all situations. This shows how every text and sermon has a b.p. and why. This leads to the critical issue of the kind of format in which all of our texts and behavioral purposes, details, associations, and vicarious experiences are expressed. The format is called a "move," and it takes place in human consciousness.

HOMILETICAL MOVES IN CONSCIOUSNESS

Homiletical moves are meaningful modules or groups of words and sentences that describe the images used to express in the concrete what we cannot adequately verbalize in the abstract. These word groups function in the traditional position held by "points," as in "three points and a poem." A move could be called a point made to come to life in human consciousness. The difference between the two formats is points are made to score in the intellect while moves involve the whole person in experiential encounters of body-strength emotion, intuition, mental processes, and spirit. Jesus' affirmation of the lawyer's words in Luke 10:27 would suggest that, far from being overly ambitious, the goal of a move in total consciousness is where God intended it to be all along: "Thou shalt love the Lord thy God with all thy heart, and with all thy soul, and with all thy strength, and with all thy mind."

The task of the move is to form and describe known images that convey parallel or metaphoric meanings, otherwise beyond clarity in direct, literal abstractions. It would seem that Jesus used parables for this reason. How do you say what compassion is, in the abstract? Only by means of visualizing a person (or a picture story thereof) being compassionate. So Jesus told a parable of a compassionate Samaritan (Luke 10:25-37).

There are a lot of fascinating angles about the priest and the church, or the race and culture of the Samaritan. However, a singular b.p. is unmistakably clear: be ye kind and generous. Don't be concerned about a person's race or class, or how that person treats your group, or how big a chunk it will add to your credit card balance when you do the final numbers at checkout time.

The moves needed to tell this story are like the progression of acts in a play:

Move I	Topic Sentence: A certain man fell among thieves.
Move II	Topic Sentence: Two churchmen passed him by.
Move III	Topic Sentence: A Samaritan stopped and aided the man.
Move IV	(The sermon celebration will be discussed in chapter 3.)

It is obvious that the above moves require submoves, each with its own topic sentence. The submoves written for Move III would include the following:

Submove A	Subtopic Sentence: Samaritan treated the victim, disregarding danger.
Submove B	Subtopic Sentence: Samaritan carried victim to care, blood stains and all.
Submove C	Subtopic Sentence: Samaritan guaranteed hostel bill.

Each position on the outline, so far, is a move or a submove in consciousness. Each has a topic sentence, and the rest of the move spells out in detail the images needed to cover that topic or subtopic before a concluding sentence. For instance, details in A could include caves in rock formations where thieves could still be hiding, and in B, the churchmen in the parable could refer to this risk for an excuse not to stop and help. Thus is illustrated the fact that each move in a series should be somehow related to moves both before and after, in addition to doing what its own topic sentence promises.

This set of required topic sentences is true of all moves, not just the story or narrative moves just discussed. The same pattern is seen in a metaphor outline on salt (Matt. 5:13), built on increments of meaning:

Move I	Topic Sentence: Salt improves the taste, making eating more pleasant.
Move II	Topic Sentence: Salt preserves, preventing the forces of decay.
Move III	Topic Sentence: Salt gives itself completely, never to return to the shaker.

Expository sermons also are designed from moves in consciousness built on increments of meaning as drawn from such sources as the linguistic analysis of the sermon text. These will be dealt with in more detail in chapter 9 on expository preaching. Meanwhile, it might do well to explain what an "increment of meaning" might be, showing these increments in the moves in consciousness in a sermon on Romans 8:28 on the providence of God:

Move I	Topic Sentence: God works in everything.
Move II	Topic Sentence: God works altogether for the good of the called.
Move III	Topic Sentence: God reserves the authority to squeeze good from deeds of most evil intent (Gen. 50:20).
Move IV	(Celebration and added subtext described in chapter 3.)

In all of these moves in consciousness there is included an introduction of an image, a sufficiently vivid description of that image for its formation in the consciousness of the congregation; direct or implicit meaning for human behavior; and a sentence of summary and transition to the next move. The first or topic sentence should also have had some low-key reference to the previous move for ease of flow. Some moves may accomplish all of this in one paragraph, but many will take several paragraphs to complete the homiletic move. In neither case should transition take away from the imagery by drawing separate attention. This attempt to keep transition in low profile is simply a way of avoiding jarring abruptness in the transition from one form in consciousness to another.

It may surprise many that so much attention is given to imagery and its formation in consciousness. After all, "This is not the gospel, is it?" Or, "Who cares what kinds of sentences are used to open and close a move?" The answer to such challenges may be simple, but it has a hard time forming in common consciousness. As has been said here, the truth is that all our "memory tapes" are in color, not in glowing grammar and rhetoric. If preachers were to strictly avoid these pictures and action stories, the hearers would be stripped of any way of recalling sermons or of retaining materials for discussion. The power of the delivery may be remembered far more than the substance, if any. And even the remembrance of rhetoric will be in pictures. A popular report has been heard for generations: "I can't remember what his text was, but he sure did preach!"

Up to this point, the ever-present element of emotion in preaching has been carefully avoided. This has not been because of lesser importance, but rather because it is such a large topic and of such importance as to demand treatment in a separate chapter. Emotion in its many phases is the subject of the chapter that follows.

NOTE

1. "Oprah Talks to Barack Obama," *O, The Oprah Magazine*, November 2004, 290.

CHAPTER 3

Emotion, Timing, and Celebration

Emotion (not *emotionalism*) is a very vital part of all human experience. Emotions surely loom large in preaching. Yet until relatively recently this topic has been avoided in the learned discussions of homiletics. In the study of other forms of human communication, the levels of emotional involvement are carefully appraised in everything from children's books to liquor ads. Levels of attention are gauged and timed; and this is about the involvement of emotions. The artistic pattern of closing a symphony with a climactic crescendo is about intentionally raising levels of emotion. By whatever name and in whatever form, concluding emotion is fine art, a vital option for preaching also.

The statistically documented decline of worship attendance in American churches is undoubtedly chargeable in significant part to loss of interest in the preaching. Sermons don't "move" people like sermons once did. Need one be reminded that preachers still hope to be "moving," but find it difficult to compete with the emotions in the media? There is more freedom in the media, while there are supposed restrictions on pulpits. ("Preachers should be more dignified.") We need to rethink the status, form, and role of passion in preaching. So the first of the four components of chapter 3 is just that: the place of passion in preaching.

The other three components are: the nature of attention and interest; the content and timing of emotional impact; and the celebration of text and purpose (ecstatic reinforcement). In all of these, the aim is to enhance the experiential encounter with the Word, with no assumption whatever that this is merely a formula for control. It is only a setting for the action of the Spirit.

THE PLACE OF PASSION IN PREACHING

Before we rethink passion as a component of modern preaching, we need to look briefly at emotion as an historical issue in Western culture. In other words, we are oddly obligated to legitimate one of humanity's highest gifts. If we don't, many may fear that putting passion in a sermon outline would be like brazenly conspiring to manipulate the hidden feelings of our congregations. Euro-American Christianity has too long overlooked the fact that Paul's famous "faith, hope, and love . . . these three," are all *emotions* (1 Cor. 13:13 NRSV). So also is trust an emotion, the prelude to obedience. There are some lower emotions like fear and hate, but there are also higher emotions like courage and unspeakable joy. Mainline Christian congregations need to open the gates of worship to that joy.

The question today is not yes or no to emotion; it is *what* emotions? And *how shall we express them?* Where shall we find models for expression? And how shall we react when our very highest emotions cease to cower in the closets of our churches and come forth to compel us to relinquish dignity and control to the Holy Spirit? How shall we redefine the word *proper* from that Lutheran line about "where the gospel is properly proclaimed and the sacraments are properly administered"?

Of this we may be sure: a subsection of the rational ego is always there in the far corner of our sane spirits to keep our expressions within the reasonable bounds of our own lifelong cultural expectations. I have seen a whole congregation of habitual shouters suddenly and rationally wax silent on hearing a preacher's flights of outrageous imagination offered as from the Bible. We have nothing to fear from the powerful influence of the true Spirit on our emotions, whatever our cultural backgrounds.

In response to authentic gospel, however, authentic emotion cries out to be expressed. Containment is costly. In fact, "emotion" comes into being only as it is expressed. The intellectual acceptance of love is not the same thing as the actual living of the gift of God called "love." Nor is the theoretical desire to experience an ideal entity called "unspeakable joy" the same thing as the overflow of that joy itself. These feelings have to find a means of manifest expression or they cease to exist at all. They die.

I once heard a Black college choir sing a deeply moving gospel anthem at a Baptist biennial convention. It was sung with no embellishments and well within the bounds of Western culture. Yet it was so powerfully moving that tears flowed from the eyes of many of all races. I noticed, however, that there were some who simply gritted their teeth and turned bright red in their efforts to constrain their feelings. It was a cultural inhibition to be pitied and a joy tragically squandered.

So if, as it should, the good news of the gospel brings forth joy, the identifiable expression of that joy should be inevitable and above question. In one form or another the indescribable ecstasy of the personal presence of the Holy Spirit will either surface or subside. Culture, social class, education, and a host of more subtle influences will determine the particular form taken by the emotional expression. Cultural expectations are so complicated that no culture dares claim superiority to any other unless, of course, that culture has the gall to deny the reality and validity of any emotional expression whatsoever; and every group's genuine folk culture, at its highest and best, will have aspects of magnificent outpouring that cross over and transcend all cultural lines.

The advice given here about sermon design will cover timing and flow of feeling, but how that feeling is expressed in a given location, denomination, class, or other group designation is always a matter of choice. We can only hope, through the years, to expand the number and depth of cultural crossovers until the day when we are all one in living conditions and culture.

Such was the case at the campfire worship of 110 high school students some sixty years ago. Almost everybody there was what we call White, including the preacher. But he closed his sermon with the singing of a "crossover" spiritual; and then the group joined in: "Lord, I want to be a Christian in my heart. . . . Lord, I want to be like Jesus in my heart, in my heart." The imploring prayer-plea of that song from another culture drew tears of sincere spiritual ambition from recently rowdy teenagers; and as they walked in silence back to their cabins, not one camper was left who had failed to respond to the invitation to follow Christ.

The same in reverse was seen in Cornerstone Church in Brooklyn one Sunday in the 1960s. The 120-voice choir lost the accompaniment of its Beethoven rendition because of a sudden mechanical failure of the organ. The a cappella singing only rose to flawless higher heights; and that huge African American audience's response still raises a lump in my throat. It was an unforgettably joyous spiritual experience, Beethoven and all.

This suggests, of course, that cultural lines are not as rigid as we might once have thought. We need to raise awareness of the values of greater openness in culture. In addition to joining us together in interethnic witness, this will greatly help enrich the worship of each of the various groups. Our purpose in this work, however, deals only with the well nigh universal principles of communication into which the styles of all the various cultural groups are poured. For example, in this camp-fire sermon, an open-minded preacher moved to the edge of his culture, to the use of a "Negro spiritual." It was a point of acceptable crossover, a shift beautifully used by God in the sermon celebration. The Apostle Paul confessed to such a stance when he said that God called him to be identified culturally with all classes and cultures in order that by all these cultures and their ways of doing things he might be used to save some (1 Cor. 9:22). The cultural options are awesome once the emotional inhibitions are transcended, and we are freed of the fear of how we might violate our cultural code of behavior if moved by the Spirit.

As has been stated, common fears of the loss of normal constraint are groundless. While sane and sober we almost never exceed our deeply imbedded cultural limits, nor does the Spirit so direct us. As the Apostle Paul assured us, the Spirit is not the author of confusion (1 Cor.14: 33). There is beauty and power in the orderly increase or intensification of deep feeling in the homiletic discipline called "timing of impact."

A final phase of passion in preaching is the amazing power of sincere, passionate personal conviction. Since great faith and trust in God is a gift, not a work, we need to know as much as we can about how to cooperate with God's giving. One very important way our personal witness is used in experiential encounters could be called "spiritual contagion," or "contagion of conviction." Gut level trust is more caught than taught, and the "carriers" seldom know when they are most "infectious." It hardly needs to be said that more faith is caught from parents than from pastors because children have more exposure to their parents' levels of trust, and their parents' emotional response to stress.

It must be understood, nevertheless, that the pulpit is a pivotal place of contagious contact. Every sermon should come from the gut level convictions of the pastor, and these are transmitted without self-conscious effort. Such contagion applies, also, to laity whose joy in the Spirit overflows in spontaneous dialogic response to the sermon, and, in some cultures, in genuine, authentic shouting. Fifty years ago a sister in my parish shouted so predictably and vigorously after sermons that I received complaints. She was accused of being disruptive; but after she died, her critics complained of missing her. They hadn't realized how much she'd been through to cause her overflow, or how much the fire in her spirit had kindled theirs. Sister Perry's love and transparent trust of her Lord were missed most by her pastor.

We move now to the nature of attention and interest as a form of and index to emotional response.

THE NATURE OF ATTENTION AND INTEREST

The effectiveness of preaching can be accurately evaluated by the interest and attention of the audience. People listen carefully and pay attention to what is of concern to them, whether positively or negatively. What some chronic excuse makers explain as audience inattention because of "too much gospel truth" is all too often couched in dogmatic extractions unrelated to real need. It is a gospel devoid of images or any other means of gaining a satisfactory personal connection with what the preacher is talking about. If there is a gap between preacher and people it is the preacher's responsibility to build the bridge, both in the pulpit and in everyday ministry.

People's interest is dependent on several factors. The first of these is a clear image and the idea it expresses; otherwise there will be no interest at all. Without a clear image in the mind of the hearer there can be no instant decision as to whether there is to be either idea or interest. If the preacher speaks in abstract or general terms with no concrete details in pictures, the hearers will recognize no ideal—no pictures, no ideas.

Of course, some status seekers may be impressed with abstractions and long, polysyllabic words. They will supply their own notion of what the speaker really meant, but that will come out of the hearer's experience, not the speaker's. That may yield several different versions of what the speaker said. But the most probable result will be no version at all.

The second factor in audience interest is the familiarity discussed in chapter 1: always remember that the most important familiarity is that of the hearer, not the preacher. Whole northern, urban congregations of immigrants from the South have been drawn together on powerful, nostalgic recollections of cotton patches and mules and muddy roads. The current generation, however, may resent such. In fact, even in the old cotton belt, the machines now do the picking and mules are a distant memory. Those once powerful cotton-patch preachers, if they are still alive, will have to find workplaces and living contexts with at least some close associations for today in order to provide the clarity and familiarity of images so greatly needed. Cars, trucks, and computers are a rich source of contemporary images. So also with televised professional athletics, cooks, and beauty treatments, although I can't recommend soap operas for familiar imagery.

A third factor in the intensity of interest also hearkens back to chapter 1 and the consideration of emotions. Preachers need to anticipate the emotional response to these familiar images used, being careful to select the ones that best serve the text and the behavioral purpose of the sermon. Every image and its idea will have some level and type of emotional quotient. Some are more loaded than others, either negatively or positively. The preacher needs to fit these into the purpose and flow of the sermon.

Preaching at a Martin Luther King Jr. birthday memorial chapel service on a huge U.S. Army base, I closed with a tale about our recently adopted Korean–African American son, age four and a half. On a two-lane road in South Carolina he had thrice demanded that I drive slowly enough to keep in close sight of the lead Jeep of a military convoy. Fearing I would be late for a preaching engagement, I asked Kim why he insisted on keeping the convoy's slow pace. In his broken English he declared, "I *like* that man!" When I asked why, he appeared to be greatly surprised at my ignorance as he solemnly announced: "Soldiers that drive Jeeps give candies and gum to little children." In the sermon I improvised three more such reports, for example: "Soldiers that drive weapons carriers give baby dolls to little girls." I repeated my text about "blessed are the peacemakers" (Matt. 5:9) and sat down.

I thought little of it until my wife's report. She had sat with the commanding officer of the post, a major general, and his wife. At the account of our adopted son's impression of the role of soldiers, the general had burst out in a flood of tears. A little later he was still so moved that he had a bit of difficulty greeting me. I wish I had known the story was that powerful in that setting. It is this type of power from familiarity that needs to be recognized and so placed in the sermon as to do the greatest good. This is called "the timing of emotional impact."

THE CONTENT AND TIMING OF EMOTIONAL IMPACT

Any work of art taking place in time must include that time factor in design. As already stated, there is a sense in which a sermon is a work of art, in parallel with great dramas and symphonies. In two of these—

the acts in a drama and the homiletic moves in a sermon—the intensity of *suspense* (emotional involvement) escalates from a low-key rising of a dramatic conflict or crucial question to a peak intensity and then resolution. A sermon then concludes with the final celebration of the text and its purpose. The low-key introduction has briefly raised the issue of the sermon but scrupulously avoided solving it, saving that for last. Symphonies join sermons and dramatic plays in glorious, celebrative conclusions. Anything after that is anticlimactic. To deviate from this ascending intensity and closure tends to violate the human sense of artistic and existential sequence, and people lose interest, ceasing to pay attention.

A female seminary student, of Scottish stock, asked to have her sermon notes "looked at." She had a preaching engagement and she hadn't yet taken a course in homiletics. The first thing I noted was the moving testimony of a teenager who was terminally ill with cancer. I suggested that this story was emotionally loaded and should be reserved for the celebration at the end of the sermon. She objected strenuously; the beginning was "exactly where the story belonged chronologically." When warned that the sermon went downhill after that, the student held her ground on the basis of chronological sequence. She yielded only after being shown that four, three, two, one was just as logical as the reverse, and that nobody would be listening if she held to her plan. Against her own will, she managed to revise this jewel that was her first sermon. Her report on the actual preaching offered humble, honest gratitude for having been helped to avoid utter failure. During the preaching, she had sensed the effectiveness of the ascending impact. Her own gut response affirmed the flow, and she shuddered at the thought of what the reverse might have been like. Art has its own internal, existential logic.

On pages 23 and 24 of chapter 2, there are two sermon outlines that illustrate two kinds of timing. In the first, the parable of the good Samaritan, the narrative sets its own ascending sequence with the stages of the actions (like the acts in a play). Suspense is built on the question, Won't *anybody* actually help this poor man? The key to choice of this "hook for suspense" is to write Jesus' behavioral purpose of moving hearers to compassion as a question: Will the protagonist be compassionate and help? (cf. chapter 4). Suspense is sustained with increasing details that argue against the purpose: Can he survive losing that much blood? Who would let all those bloodstains ruin his beast's blanket? What if the same robbers are still behind the rock? His money is gone; who is going to pay the hostel bill, and how? The answers are drawn out for suspense. When the questions are finally answered, the story is over, except for the celebration. The outline might be thus:

Lesson or Pericope: Luke 10:29-37
Sermon Text: Luke 10:33b
Behavioral   To move hearers to have compassion for
Purpose: those in great need.
Move I: Thieves nearly killed a traveler on the Jericho road.
Move II: Two holy churchmen were too busy to help.
Move III: A hated Samaritan had compassion and helped the traveler.
Move IV: Jesus affirmed the Samaritan's act as truly neighborly.

The subtopics under Move III could be:

A.   The Samaritan wasn't supposed to deal with the Jews who hated him.
B.   There was reason to expect that the thieves were still behind the rock.
C.   The traveler was bloody and badly hurt, possibly dying.
D.   The traveler was as much on business and in a hurry as the churchmen.

The subtopics under Move IV would begin with the Samaritan's actions, which answer all the questions of suspense raised in Move III.

The second and more frequently used timing pattern is where the various increments of meaning in a metaphor or in an expository text are simply weighed for impact and sequenced in order of increasing emotional impact. Jesus' parable of salt is a classical example of increments of meaning to be arranged in ascending intensity:

Move I   Salt improves taste or flavor.
Move II   Salt preserves.
Move III   Salt sacrifices its all in that which it saves.

The subtopics in each of these moves bring its idea to life with illustrative materials (genres, as described in part II) of the same ascending intensity. The audience will likely fail to note this subtle sequence, but they will react with rapt attention and complimentary comments. More important are the additional responses of increased memory and changed behavior, the crowning value of all this discipline of timing and its conclusion in celebration. We turn now to the criteria of the purposefully focused emotional expression called "celebration."

THE CELEBRATION OF TEXT AND PURPOSE

The timed peak of emotional impact is climactically applied to the sermon's text and behavioral purpose in celebration. This literally serves as ecstatic reinforcement. That is, people recall best those things about which the associated emotional response was celebrative joy, along with being focused and *purposeful*. This gladness is no mere trip for "kicks"; it tends to etch into memory the substantive content. The traditionally abstract "point" in sermons takes on experiential significance. To accomplish this, there are several criteria for the celebration commonly found in moves in consciousness III or IV of a sermon.

The first of these criteria is the focus of the celebration on the sermon's text and purpose. The emotional expression of joy is focused on this achievement or fulfillment. The hearers then identify with and into that fulfillment with joy, and, by the aid of the Spirit, are changed. I recall different hero identifications at different age levels, such as David; then Daniel; then Peter, Paul, Priscilla, and others, each modeling a different goal of growth and behavior.

In 1954, when court-ordered civil rights in the schools had stirred much backlash, Gardner C. Taylor didn't argue with an audience rich in possible opposition. He painted a picture of the communion table in heaven and of the welcome given by Jesus, the host and center of the piece, to anyone. I saw ten thousand people then moved to tears by the celebration of their own communion and the vision of the countenance of Jesus. No argument could ever have moved them so. It was well over fifty years ago, but one forgets neither the celebrated scene in heaven nor the relevant scene on earth. And one can never be the same. Such is the function of true celebration.

Perhaps the greatest sin of most of the preachers I heard as a child, away from my home church, was the sin of irrelevant celebration. It was the sin of pasting on the sermon a climax known to be moving, regardless of obvious disconnection with the text. It was like putting an eraser on the main body of the sermon, because the part most responded to and best remembered would be the celebration—the "gravy." Again, it was like drowning a beef dinner in chicken gravy, as a tool for manipulated response. The truest and best gravy is made with the juice from the meat itself. The greatest and most helpful celebration is made from the essence of the text, which it powerfully affirms and renders unforgettable.

Concerning the celebration of the text, a final issue arises when there is no fittingly celebrative material in the text or lesson context from which the sermon is preached. Such is the case, for instance, when preaching on providence from Romans 8:28. The increments of meaning to be discussed later include the abstract certainty of "We know!" But this includes no pictures—no images of providence. My own favorite picture of providence is found in Genesis 50:20 and its setting. Joseph's speech about how his brothers meant it for evil but God meant it for good is profound theology of divine providence *and* classic drama for celebration. One can get celebratively happy over knowing that God doesn't *plan* evil; but God reserves the authority to squeeze a blessing out of the evil that others plan. The issue in searching outside the primary text, or its context, is to be convinced that the material imported is completely in harmony with that text and its behavioral purpose.

A second criterion is that the text and sermon maintain a predominantly positive tone—an emphasis on what the text motivates and empowers hearers to do, rather than what *not* to do. Jesus' Beatitudes are magnificently positive (Matt. 5:3-12). Jesus' parable of the empty house says it in pictures: Beware of negatively sweeping a dwelling empty and providing nothing to fill the space (Matt. 12:43-45). The good news of the gospel is exactly that: *good news.* Positive gospel is both filling and fulfilling.

Negative sermons are far easier to write, and they can sound forth with attractive certainty. It is far easier to criticize and raise questions than to offer helpful answers. Sandy F. Ray typically said it with a metaphor: "The bulldozer is the most spectacular machine in the building industry; it can destroy in three days what it took three years to build. The only trouble is that you have nothing left when it has finished." Actually, you have less than nothing; hearers are left wide open for manipulation and temptation.

Positive sermons are harder to design, especially among young preachers, but the empowerment of the positive is worth the work, as shown in the Gardner C. Taylor sermon mentioned above. Many of the sins belabored in pulpits don't really need the negative attention given them. These sins are already well known to be sins. In cases where sensitivity to transgression needs to be increased, there is a helpful rule of thumb: keep the criticism to a third or less of the total sermon and never start or finish on a negative note. Negative beginnings cancel interest and attention—they turn people off. Conclusions need to be positive, because you can't celebrate what is not positive or is not right. Any rare exceptions to this rule are where there is no celebration at all. Predominantly good news gospel is best after all.

Students often take this to mean that we suggest being soft on sin—not prophetic enough. They forget that prophets "hit and run," so to speak. They are not located pastors preaching weekly. Only sick spiritual masochists desire to be spanked spiritually every Sunday. Furthermore, sin-centered preaching keeps temptation topics in the conscious mind, without empowering one to overcome. This amounts to advertising evil and spreading it. Positive preaching fills the void and leads to the abundant living for which Christ came in the first place (John 10:10b).

Challenge or admonition must not be mistaken for celebration any more than passionate negativity. Essential elements such as rebuke and strong hints about pet sins need to be in the main body of the sermon. "Signifying" about sin does not fit in supposed celebration. Again, this may seem soft on sin, but text-centered, joyous emotion on the part of pastor and people is definitely more effective for good than challenge, no matter how forceful the critical rhetoric.

Not that sermons should never challenge; quite the contrary. Sermons should always admonish and motivate people to climb to higher ground, but never with direct "we oughts," and never in the celebration. Hearers don't rejoice about what they know they ought to be doing and aren't doing. However, they can be lured and joyously led to *seek* higher ground on their own initiative. They can be transformed, in the moment of greatest spiritual joy, about what God has done in Christ and can do in them. And they go home different from what they were when they came.

To the rule of timed ascending of impact there needs to be added the further rule of reserving the peak experience for the celebration. There should be only one peak experience, and it should be in the concluding celebration. More than one peak renders the second peak anticlimactic. The Spirit willing, it is at this one point that the spiritual transformation of persons most often takes place.

The particular style taken for the peak is culturally determined. In some settings, the peak is characterized by the loudest sounds of the service. In other groups, utter silence is cherished at the peak, and the prevailing intensity in that silence is awesome. The one aspect held in common is that neither shouting Baptists nor silent Quakers nor all in between should seek summary of the sermon at the celebrative point. What is sought is symbolic centering on experiential encounter, not essay-style intellectual summation.

There is yet another rule that guides good celebration. It is called "heightened rhetoric." It has verbal impact not heard in the main body of the sermon, but reserved for the celebration. When out of this place it sounds like overkill, but it serves beautifully at the peak. Whatever follows it, other than closure, is anticlimactic.

It is the style of David singing, "Surely goodness and mercy shall follow me all the days of my life: and I will dwell in the house of the LORD for ever" (Psalm 23:6). It is Paul's rhetorical question and answer: "Who shall separate us from the love of Christ? . . . For I am persuaded, that neither death, nor life, nor angels, nor principalities, nor powers, nor things present, nor things to come, Nor height, nor depth, nor any other creature, shall be able to separate us from the love of God, which is in Christ Jesus our Lord" (Rom. 8:35a, 38-39). It is the rhetoric of Abraham Lincoln at Gettysburg, or Martin Luther King Jr. at Washington, D.C., with "I have a dream."

This is the emotionally loaded language of the soul in celebration. It flattens out if used for too long a stretch; but whether it is the words of a great hymn, poem, drama, or, supremely, the Bible, heightened rhetoric is large enough to express adequately what the soul aflame cries out to say. The flaming tongues of the celebrating servant, who has already grasped and accepted the text and its behavioral purpose, warm its now frequent abstractions.

A final criterion or rule of celebration is drawn from the already discussed influence of spiritual contagion. Great preaching, and celebration in particular, is best done by preachers who embody the very trust to which they would draw the hearer.

Audiences receive most the message that comes not only from lofty words, but also from the very soul of the preacher. It is impossible fully to imitate the unspeakable joy of the soul set free. The deep and abiding trust in providence discussed earlier is more caught than taught.

It was parents' weekend on the campus of a small, church-founded, women's college. The chapel was more full than ever as I took my text in Ezekiel 3:15: "I sat where they sat." The b.p. was to be used of the Spirit to close the generation gap between parents and teens, which was so rampant in the 1960s. The genre (covered in part II, chapter 5) of the sermon was a character sketch of Ezekiel. He embodied the change of heart from judgmental to understanding and remedy, as seen in the text, by sitting where "they" (both students and parents, of whom I was one) sat. The outline was, briefly:

Move I   Ezekiel went to the captives at Telabib in judgmental anger.

Move II   Ezekiel spent seven days observing their situation.

Move III   Ezekiel contributed huge new insights to Old Testament religion.

Move IV   Celebrate the mind of Christ, which is to sit where we sit.

(Phil. 2:5: "Let this mind be in you, which was also in Christ Jesus.")

The response of the parents was warm and often tearful, but the surprise was in the students. They, too, had identified into the prophet, and they could see why their parents felt as they did. In a word, they all celebrated the principle of sitting where others sit, even when it costs as much as it cost our Lord.

We turn now to part II and the tools that provide formats for these experiential encounters with the Word. These tools implement the preacher's high calling. The purposes of love and trust and compassion move from abstraction to action in concrete contexts of experience; these contexts or formats are called "genres." The most common of these genres is the narrative, the story. There are several others and many combinations.

PART II

GENRES: THE VEHICLES OF EXPERIENCE

We have seen that abstract ideas or doctrines become moves in consciousness only after being embodied in a concrete parallel from *experience*. Love is known in an *act* of love. In turn, experience can't be in the abstract either. It has to have some concrete image of action in the sermon. The expression that emotion requires has to occur in concrete experience also, in some known and accepted format of behavior or literary genre. As already stated, Jesus' parables served these purposes with an array of images of actions, of metaphors and similes, all parallel to the abstract. These were often couched in story form. Jesus was never without such imagery in his preaching and teaching, according to Matthew, Mark, and Luke. All of Jesus' different kinds of parables are called genres; and there are several more. Every preacher needs to know which genre or combination of genres to select to make each text's idea come alive in the consciousness of the hearer.

The genres covered in part II are as follows, each in a separate chapter: Chapter 4, on the narrative and related forms, deals with the many uses of the story form, such as the monologue, the personal testimony, the character impersonation, the dialogue, and the news report. Chapter 5 deals with the character sketch and related forms, always applied to one person. These are combinations of small story bits or scenes about one person, each illustrating a similar personal characteristic. Chapter 6 deals with the same kinds of briefer sketches as chapter 5, except that they are applied to *groups* of people, rather than individuals. The title of chapter 6 is "Variations on the Group Study." All three of these chapters, 4 to 6, describe some type of narrative; whether long or short, each has or implies the narrative elements of b.p., protagonist, conflict, and resolution.

Chapters 4 to 6 in part II are basically narrative; so also is chapter 9 on the stream of consciousness. Chapter 7 is on parables, metaphors, and similes, and chapter 8 is on expository preaching and the combination of genres in one sermon.

The choice of which genre to use depends on the sermon text and its context in Scripture. When the text line is imbedded in a complete narrative, the choice is obvious. The parable of the prodigal son is a *narrative*. But if the story line in a parable is altogether too brief to be enlarged, or if there is no story at all, another genre for the sermon's main body is indicated. For instance, the parable of the prodigal son (Luke 15:11-24), Jesus' most important theologically, gives easily enough story detail for elaboration into a twenty-minute narrative sermon. It practically demands a full-story treatment in a sermon.

In contrast, the parable of the new patch and the old garment has minimal action (Luke 5:36) and no suspense. A genre other than a story or narrative is required. In this case it is a metaphor, with stages of the stitching as increments of symbolic meaning and moves in consciousness. The subtopics elaborate on meaning rather than on narrated stages of action.

In this parable one also has to shift the story from negative (about what a man does not do) to positive. The outline might look like this:

Text and Lesson:	Luke 5:36a: "No man putteth a piece of a new garment upon an old."
Behavioral Purpose:	To move hearers to accept new practices and discard dead traditions.
Genre:	Metaphor: Implied actions are used in outline as increments of symbolic meaning.

I. All garments show worn places and holes from long use.
   A. Good garments wear well in the beginning.
   B. Certain religious traditions served well in their beginning.
   C. Wear and tear is inevitable, not disgraceful.
II. Worn garments cannot accept patches of new material.
   A. Well-meaning people desire to patch with new material.
   B. Devout believers seek to save old institutional practice with new ideas.
   C. The new patches don't match and so tear out larger holes.
III. It is best to start over with all new material.
   A. Prudent people just buy a new garment.
   B. The wise and faithful accept outright new practices offered by Jesus.
   C. The fresh and new practices can be enjoyed and celebrated.

Choices will have to be made if several different genres happen to appear in a first-flow draft of inspiration for a sermon. As will be seen in chapter 9, the genre selected and followed should be the genre closest to the main *structure* of the whole sermon. The preacher should then make sure the whole sermon is consistent with this form, with other genres fitting into the various subfoci. The purpose of making this firm choice is not a matter of being "proper"; it is a matter of making sure that the sermon fits and flows together and can be followed easily in the hearer's mind.

Two more kinds of problems choosing genre can appear if a preacher is working on 1 Thessalonians 5:18. The first kind of challenge could occur if the preacher stumbled onto the dramatic example of Paul on trial before King Agrippa: "I think myself happy" (Acts 26:2). One could easily be tempted to abandon the original text (1 Thess. 5:18) altogether and preach a narrative sermon on Acts 26:2. The b.p. would be the same: giving thanks in *every*thing. Greater elaboration would then be placed on cuff irons and leg chains and on Paul's status as a common criminal, with his happiness nonetheless.

The second challenge with 1 Thessalonians 5:18 (a four-word text, "In everything give thanks") arises directly from the fact that it is so abstract. Its context offers no suggestions whatsoever on genre. The traditional solution would be a sermon of expository genre, built on increments of meaning motivating gratitude. The more creative solution would be a character sketch of Paul as a person vividly embodying the text. As we shall see in chapter 5, this genre is a series of real-life encounters, making the four-word, abstract text come alive with moves of suspense: "Will Paul be able to give thanks *here*?" The first sketch would be the hearing in Agrippa's court. Quite obviously, this latter option is far superior to a traditional "three points and a poem" sermon, because of the maintaining of suspense, interest, and attention.

One more type of challenge in choice of genre is seen in Romans 8:28, the text on providence mentioned above. In this case, the genre actually chosen first was traditional expository, as described in chapter 9. Moves are developed from *linguistic analysis* of the text into interesting increments of meaning. The preacher's challenge then is to illustrate each move with a fascinating story, metaphor, or other image. The first choice made was not to stay as abstract as the text and main moves. The subgenres chosen for each move are shown in chapter 9. The main moves chosen were as follows, based on linguistic analysis of Romans

8:28a: "And we know that all things are worked together for good to them that love God" (author's translation).

Move I   Topic Sentence: God works in *everything*.
Move II   Topic Sentence: God always works for good.
Move III   Topic Sentence: God's blessing happens regardless of seeming odds. (Can be used as celebration, eliminating Move IV.)
Move IV   Topic Sentence: We *celebrate* this certainty: We KNOW!

The most challenging of the genres in part II is probably the "stream of consciousness." It requires the poetic subjectivity of David. Yet no preacher should escape this challenge and forfeit the potential power of this genre. One just has to identify with David for a while and follow David's mood to the celebrative end in excerpts from such a psalm as the fifty-first. The concluding celebrative move would come from verse 15 ("my mouth shall shew forth thy praise") or verse 19 ("then shalt thou be pleased).

Good preaching is blessed by the varieties of style that come from familiarity with *all* of the genres described here. No preacher is equally good at all the genres, but a sincere and disciplined effort to maintain variety is always an appreciated improvement.

We turn now to the efforts of this author to embody the advice offered here in genres that will cause the task of sermon design to become both satisfying and abundantly fruitful, in addition to being challenging.

CHAPTER 4

The Narrative and Related Forms

The most frequently used genre is the narrative or story. This genre includes a number of variations on the theme of telling interesting, purposeful gospel tales. The principles on which stories operate have been explained already. Each story has a protagonist or main character who lives out the *behavioral purpose* (b.p.)[1] of the text. This person is confronted with a conflict, question, plot, or issue that is the behavioral purpose written as a question: Will this protagonist fulfill this behavioral purpose? The resolution of conflict, or answer to this question after buildup of suspense, is: Yes, the Samaritan *will* have compassion (or whatever the b.p. question happens to be). The story then is over and there is nothing left to do but celebrate the victory. This intentionally focused joy hopefully inspires the hearer to remember and live by the b.p. for the rest of the hearer's life.

The transformative power of the story lies in the hearer's identification with the main character and her or his vicarious appropriation and practice of the behavior sought. In other words, the hearer aspires to be like the hero or heroine who lives up to the b.p. If there is more than one different protagonist in the story the preacher has to select only one or one group. This choice of main characters can't be done, of course, until after the b.p. has been chosen.

The parable of the prodigal son contains at least two, maybe three, "good guys": the gracious father, the prodigal son, and possibly the elder brother. Jesus probably assumed the father to be chief character but implying the son's acceptance of parental forgiveness as his b.p. Most preachers today choose the son, taking the son's repentant return home as the b.p. The older son parable is incomplete. In the other two the b.p. would be chosen first, and choice of main character would follow automatically. The conflict in the first would have been, Will the father actually forgive and receive the son? In the latter, the question or conflict would have been, Will the son repent and go back home?

This choice of b.p. and matching protagonist determines how the same story will be told: in which of two different ways, for two different purposes, with two different resolutions. If fatherly forgiveness is the purpose, when this has been granted or recounted (Luke 15:22-24) the resolution has taken place and the story is over. If the repentant return of the son is the purpose, the resolution occurs when the return has been described (Luke 15:18-19). Both possible resolutions are followed by joyous celebration of the b.p.: the father's forgiveness, in the first version, or the son's repentant return in the second.

A third option bends the formula a bit but fits the record of the trilogy of Jesus' parables. This approach takes the parable as Jesus' all-important portrayal of the unconditional grace of God, which is then celebrated in the final move. Although heaven's joy is not mentioned after the lost son parable, parallel joy in heaven is connected with the finding of both the lost sheep and the lost coin (vv. 7 and 10). This clearly justifies the concluding celebration of God's grace in a sermon on the parable of the lost son.

Of course, there are many other variations on this parable; one hermeneutics class found more than fifty. Included were many imaginative renditions, such as the story told as the son's personal testimony; as a father's monologue as he scanned the horizon, looking for his son; and as if the story occurred in the twentieth century. In this case, the son went to Wall Street and blew his bundle on public relations, after which his friends and potential mentors promptly abandoned him.

A seminary student in Los Angeles preached this parable in a youth revival. In his version, the son's hunger was discovered in the empty refrigerator of a UCLA student. In the refrigerator were only a bottle of tap water and a sleeve of soda crackers, as found by the student's parents when they came to visit their sick son. The options for relevant identification in this parable are awesome when sought with inspired creativity.

In all these versions the preacher was careful not to vilify the son or portray him as a wretched ingrate. This would have prevented the youths in the audience from identifying with the protagonist. He had to be portrayed as a decent kid who just needed to find himself, like many of the youths in the audience. The family in Jesus' parable fitted the affluent middle-class families in this Los Angeles audience: second sons often had no responsibility and very few challenges for fulfillment or reason to become mature. The preacher, then, was free to see the son as immature rather than evil. Luke's version of the parable in the Scriptures left ample literal space for any "loose-leaf kid in Los Angeles."

PERSONAL TESTIMONY: CONVERSION STORY

Far and away the most common variation on the basic narrative structure is the personal testimony of how one was saved. Almost any sincere and candid testimony can draw interest, whether by laity or by clergy. Audiences identify into testimonies because most hearers will have some form of personal parallel. The story of the day the preacher was "born again" never fails to move hearers, especially when used in the celebration of a well-timed sermon. However, stories glorifying "me" must be avoided. The main suggestion to be offered here has to do with the obligation to follow the disciplines of timing and focus. A personal testimony of conversion, or of any other experience, is not a meandering stream; it is still a structured gospel sermon with a text, a behavioral purpose, a suspense-producing conflict, and a resolution.

PERSONAL TESTIMONY: EYEWITNESS

The rules apply also to all narration to which the preacher is an eyewitness. Unless there are constraints of such things as professional confidence, if the preacher actually saw the story happen, the story is always better told as an eyewitness account. Another advantage arises out of the already mentioned fact that hearers remember in pictures. So also do preachers. This means that communication can be much more effective because there is no need for a manuscript. With good memory and eye contact and better access to one's own depths, eyewitness testimony, when guided by discipline, is a treasure indeed.

There are, however, things to beware of. One is the tendency to tell it always with "me" as the protagonist. Then the glory goes to the preacher and not to God. Unless the preacher's role in the tale is very humbling, it is best to avoid self in eyewitness. It is even wise to keep self to a minimum in all the action seen as an eyewitness when one is in the same pulpit Sunday after Sunday.

Eyewitness testimony is best indulged in as it concerns places and people away from the present parish. Great illustrations need to be preserved for later use. The ploy of names disguised in the same parish often fails. People recognize their own problem no matter what fictitious name or place, if any, is attached.

A final word of advice here involves the need to maintain a disciplined reading schedule of the Bible and the classics, as well as the media and scholarly works. One needs a variety of sources for illustration: one's personal experiences are not an endless or inexhaustible resource, nor would the audience wish them to be. Between the extremes of frigid aloofness and overexposure lies a happy medium in which people get an accurate and discretely open image of their pastor.

MONOLOGUE AND CHARACTER IMPERSONATION

The second most common variation on the narrative is the impersonation of characters from the Bible, or from public or personal history, in a monologue. Usually done in costume, this dramatic presentation is used both as a sermon and, often, as a church-school lesson. In a sermon, dramatization of persons is too often done without the narrative structure, conflict, and suspense. The impressiveness of the costumes and the dramatization of emotional scenes suffice to impress most hearers. But the potential effectiveness is wasted without the structure, focus, and flow of a whole narrative. The b.p. is lost in an effort to deal with the whole life rather than to focus on pertinent details, timing, and a celebration of a text.

One of the most memorable impersonations I ever heard was when E. K. Bailey launched an impersonation with a low-voiced, resonant announcement: "My name is Hosea." His casual-sounding report of the odd details of what God directed him to do gained a truly tight grip on the audience's attention.

DIALOGUE

In recent years, my wife and I have been frequently invited to preach in dialogue. Finding no guidelines in print, we have had to generate some. The first guideline is that the material must be written to *flow between* the two preachers. This, as opposed to dialogue with the audience, leaves them overhearing our conversation. We are not just taking turns reading a sermon. Two personalities must be reflected in interaction, in addition to the standard narrative requirements.

Whenever possible, they should identify with opposite sides of an issue, at least until the arrival of the resolution. The parts taken should be in harmony with the personalities and interests of the person reading. For instance, where children were at issue in the dialogue, the advocate assigned was the specialist with children whom I married sixty-four years ago—my wife. Where dialogue needed debate, and one side was "unChristian," the written part allowed the person on the "wrong" side to move out of negative character before the celebration. Sometimes such a character can be redeemed beforehand with such a disclaimer as, "Let me play devil's advocate for a moment."

The resolution always brings the conversers together, and both join in the celebration. Whatever is necessary should be done to make this credible. There are many dialogues, however, in which both speakers are on the same side, viewing the same action. Dialogue does not necessarily require an antagonist to go with the protagonist. In such a case, the variety is generated from slightly different or supplementary views of the same story as viewed by the contrasting personalities.

The description of *impersonation* could have included impersonations of more than one speaker. We have enacted Jesus and the woman at the well (John 4:7-15), which is a dialogue; and there are many other biblical dialogues. Of course, there are also imaginative dialogues such as the chat I had with King David during a privileged brief visit "on high." I asked him how in the world, after some of his deeds, he got to be recorded as a "man after [God's] own heart" (Acts 13:22). This drew great interest during the administration of President Clinton. The answer from David was found in his spirit, as expressed in Psalm 51.

MEDIA NEWS REPORT

Imaginative news reports have been used to stir rapt attention. This is not so much for the newspaper angle as for the reporter's style of dealing with exciting, often tragic news. On-the-spot, eyewitness description, doubled with the staccato delivery of a journalist, can draw an audience's intense interest—but not for too long. A full sermon in this style would be a form of overkill, but smaller news bits can be very effective.

Newsform, then, is a way of telling a story; but it can't be a whole story with all the bells and whistles. Its brief style itself creates the needed feeling of suspense. The news media style can add some spice, but always within limits.

The narrative category thus includes any tale or testimony that has a main character, a conflict or plot, and some form of resolution. Most of the crucial aspects of the process apply: identification with a familiar main character and maintenance of an ascending level of suspense. If parts of these elements are crowded out in a brief format, they still apply by implication. Of course, the one celebration covers all, and the whole package is justified by the fact that the celebration of the text and its purpose gives focus and ecstatic reinforcement for application of the purpose to real life.

RULES OF NARRATIVE FOCUS

In the just concluded varieties of narrative it was always stated that, regardless of the many variations, if there was a story it had to follow narrative rule. These rules were to be found here and there. This is to supply a code summation for handy reference:

1. The behavioral purpose (b.p.) is usually drawn from the sermon's scriptural text or from the pericope of the lesson in the order of service. However, the b.p. may be more clearly stated in another place in the Bible.
2. The protagonist of every story is the person who fulfills its behavioral purpose. The narrator never says this, but this fulfillment is precisely why the sermon is preached.
3. The plot or issue question in the story is the basis for the suspense that causes the rapt attention needed for identification and transformation. This question is always, Will the protagonist accomplish the behavioral purpose of the text?
4. The resolution of the conflict is always the answer *yes,* and the celebration is always centered on this accomplishment.

The "always" factor is not to suggest that every narrator should sound the same. Quite the contrary; these are generic guidelines of process, without which the hearers' attention will be directed to purposes other than those of the sermon. In addition, any other means of success in holding attention will only undermine the biblically based purpose of the sermon. Every preacher who follows this structure and process will still have to supply a cultural and/or personal style of design writing and delivery.

A CLARIFICATION OF NARRATIVE TYPOLOGIES

It is bound to occur to some of the readers of this detailed study of storytelling that there are some highly respected critics of narratives in preaching. What, then, can be said to resolve this difference among responsible scholars and others who bear the awesome burden of communicating a word from the Word that saves and nurtures growth?

First of all, we need to be sure we are talking about the same thing. The storytelling treated here is not some rare gift given only to a blessed few or to certain ethnic groups. It is a skill amenable to analysis and teachable to normally capable students. One may still learn storytelling by the folk method of intuition, but this takes years too long; and the resultant skills don't include the capacity to select from a variety of behavioral goals. To be sure, storytelling is best done in the casual folk style, as opposed to learned lecture formality, but style of delivery can be practiced and learned also.

The storytelling described here is certainly not the same storytelling so rightly opposed by David Buttrick in his classic *Homiletic:* "Nevertheless, though storytelling from the pulpit may entertain, excite, and inform, it does not necessarily shape faith-consciousness. Story qua story may not be an adequate preaching."[2] The stories opposed tend to be used for "warm-ups," attention getters for the speaker rather than for the Word of God. Of course, this may be a legitimate purpose so long as it is fully understood that this is not in the sermon: "He ain't took his text yet." Once the sermon is launched, the storytelling should be focused to serve the text and b.p. only.

Buttrick's comment goes on to express approval of the storytelling of a "skilled Black preacher." Although my description of this tradition does not match his verbatim, it is unquestionably true that we both consider this tradition to be a useful source for effective preaching models for the future. Indeed, this is precisely what this book attempts to do. Usually the orderly issues of focus are not consciously dealt with in Black tradition, but even this vital concern can often be detected as the Spirit supplements intuitive tendencies to relate to gospel goals.

The sum and substance of it all is that narration is desperately needed to help bring alive the moribund pulpits of today. The goals are not only the saving of souls and their nurture for spiritual growth; the resurrection of whole congregations as the body of Christ is at stake. The so-called narrative theology in the parables does in fact enlighten learned doctrine, but it is a mistake to suppose that Jesus' goals in the parables were primarily doctrinally enlightening rather than holistically behavioral. The time has come when preaching pastors simply must endure the hardship of overcoming cultural inhibitions and learn skills that the pulpit needs perhaps more than at any point in modern history.

The following chapter on personality sketches includes many mini narratives, rather than just one full-length account, but the same enlivening applies. The power of this genre is in its concentration on the characteristics of one person, helping that person become vividly alive in the consciousness of the hearer.

NOTES

1. It is interesting to observe that a top authority on screenwriting, Robert McKee, urges the same need for purpose in his book *Story: Substance, Style and the Principles of Screenwriting* (New York: ReganBooks, 1997), pages 33 and 138. The desire and drive of McKee's protagonists is the same as the behavioral purpose of protagonists in this book. In both cases suspense is built on the question of whether they'll succeed in this purpose.

2. David Buttrick, *Homiletic: Moves and Structures* (Philadelphia: Fortress Press, 1987), 335.

CHAPTER 5

The Character Sketch
and Related Forms

The genre called "character sketch" is a series of episodes or scenes from the life of a protagonist, each scene illustrating the same or a similar characteristic of that person. This trait is always the same as the behavioral purpose drawn from the text. This arrangement thus uses the personality of the hero or heroine of the story to draw the hearer into the desire to live by that same biblically guided behavior. This is accomplished by means of the hearers' admiring and willing identification with the protagonist or hero, who already emulates and lives by that text-based purpose.

The protagonist's character and personality are not described in adjectives such as *kind*, or *hard working*, since memory is retained in pictures, not words. The sketch is written to portray the personality in word pictures about the smiling countenance or the bent-over back. The image is also heard in the voice, and seen in concrete behavior. Details like "Samaritan" are essential to build the image of a real person in the mind of the hearer; but the most important details have to do with feelings and attitudes behind that behavior. It is the *character* or *personality* as model that is being sketched.

Lest this appear to be what a clinical psychologist might call a "behaviorist" definition, it must be understood that this identification process is not at all an attempt at mechanistic control. No preacher using the most vivid and interesting sketches of character can predict what any one hearer will do in response. Effective sermons must be focused, nonetheless, on a single behavior for literary reasons. The fact is that the only specific result to be anticipated is the attention given to an engaging sermon, made easy to follow by its organization around a single theme and behavioral purpose and its timed flow up to celebration. One preacher plants, but doesn't stand by and expect that he or she will be able to see instant growth. Another waters, but is likewise limited in how much can be seen on the spot. If there is to be any increase it will be *God* who gives it, and in God's own time (1 Cor. 3:6; cf. chapter 11).

Another metaphor relevant to character-sketch preaching (and all other genres) is to be found in Isaiah's urgent call: "Prepare ye the way of the LORD, make straight in the desert a highway for our God" (Isa. 40:3). We preachers dare not take credit. It doesn't matter how many converts are saved as we preach, or how many are led to abundant life. We dare claim no more specific influence than that it was easier for seekers to find God on "the path that I helped clear of stones and mud holes and intellectual obstacles." One professor advised us to labor arduously as if it were all in our hands. We should then trust, knowing it was all in God's hands. We need to use all of these topic and subtopic sentences as instruments in the hands of God.

MONOLOGUE

The most obvious as well as most popular variation on the character sketch is the autobiographical sketch. It differs from the personal (as eyewitness) testimony in the previous chapter in that the autobiographical sketch is about *traits of the speaker* rather than the acts or traits of a third person such as Abraham. Acts 26:4-19 portrays Paul using as a defense his personal testimony of his own *acts* (see previous chapter) to illustrate his *trait* (see this chapter) of faithfulness to the leading of God. It may not seem to matter greatly which way one classifies this story, but often the choice is important (part II, p. 41). This incident is cited in the context of a sermon on thanksgiving. Although Paul used it as a character reference in court, the court scene is only one of several episodes where Paul's thankfulness is evident. The four-word text and the b.p. are stated the same way.

Text and Lesson:	1 Thess. 5:18 ("In every thing give thanks") and Acts 26:2-27.
Behavioral Purpose:	To be used to move hearers to give thanks in all things.
Introduction:	Imaginary dialogue with Paul regarding challenge of text and Paul's embodiment.
Move I	Paul lives up to his rigorous b.p. in Agrippa's court.
Move II	Paul stands the test again in the jail at Philippi.

| Move III | Paul stands the test at Rome, with awesome impact on missions. |
| Move IV | To my surprise, I gave thanks during surgery on my own heart (Celeb). |

The following transcript of this sermon as preached will flesh out the way this outline and many of the supporting details looked at full length, including the sometimes questioned use of imagination to dramatize issues and gain rapt attention.

THANKS IN EVERYTHING? (SAMPLE SERMON)

In every thing give thanks: for this is the will of God in Christ Jesus concerning you. (1 Thess. 5:18)

Introduction

I don't seem to pay much attention to Thessalonians until Thanksgiving, when I need a text for the season. Paul's word is very handy, but this year that text seems for some reason to go to more extremes than usual. The Apostle Paul is often heard to say things like this, but this year I got the feeling that he was very serious. I asked, "Brother Paul, do you really mean to say *every?*" He answered, "Yesss! *Every* thing!"

I said, "But that seems a bit much. It evokes the same response I give to religious fanatics. You're a thoughtful and reasonable man. Are you serious?" He simply said, "Serious as a heart attack." When he saw how surprised I was, he added, "But notice I said *in*, not *for*." I protested, "That's still extreme, don't you think?" He grumbled a bit, saying, "That's what I said, and that's what I meant." Then he challenged me to look at his record and see if he practiced what he so pointedly preached—to see if, as we say, he put his money where his mouth was.

Move 1

It turns out that Paul is thankful no matter how difficult the situation. He writes the Philippians, "I thank my God upon every remembrance of you" (1:3). That's typical of Paul but strange, generally speaking. Don't you know that Philippi is where Paul got thrown in jail for healing that girl who told fortunes? Not only that, but also he and his party were stripped and *beaten* before they were incarcerated! I would think Paul would wish to forget a place like that. But even in the solitary confinement of the inner prison, with their hands and feet in the stocks, unable to ward off rats or insects, Paul and his friend were actually singing and praising God. In other words, even in the midst of the darkness, dampness, and danger of a dungeon, they *thanked* God (Acts 16:22-24). Wow!

I can't imagine what they were praising God for, unless it was for just being alive. Maybe it was like the slaves who thanked God that their bed was not their cooling board, and their cover was not their winding sheet—for being clothed in their right minds. I guess if you've got enough breath to cry and complain, you've got *some*thing to be thankful for. Whatever the basis, Paul didn't stop thanking God under even the worst conditions.

Move 2

Occasionally one can hear Paul stating why. It may be subtle, and it is ingenious, but it is definitely thanks. Acts 26:2-27 finds Paul, as it were, in handcuffs and leg irons, a common convict hailed before King Agrippa's court. He is an accused prisoner, but he is also a Roman citizen, so the court informs him that he is now permitted to speak for himself. The words that come out are in the tested terminology of the court, as we say. It is legal and polite to begin with the words, "I consider myself happy, O King Agrippa, that I am privileged to answer for myself this day before you concerning all those grave charges that have been lodged against me by the Jews." It is a noble statement, worthy of a man with Paul's training, but how do you go about making it sound so very sincere? Here you are preaching the very gospel of our Lord, and yet you are treated as a common criminal! Surely there is nothing to be thankful about in this crushing defeat of high idealism.

The answer is in between the lines. Paul is saying that he is happy to be in a jurisdiction that gives each person his or her day in court. He is into the proper recognition of the fact that Rome guarantees him due process. He is also delighted to have the hearing before a man known for his unusual familiarity with the customs and questions at issue. However, this is only the first and literal, or surface meaning, of this courtly address.

Paul in his heart is thanking God that he has this opportunity to speak to a *king!* Agrippa is wearing two hats. He is a sitting judge, but he is also a reigning king. Some people live all their lives and never get to speak or preach or testify before a king.

Furthermore, most kings can get bored or tired and simply say, "Away with him!" Or they can "turn it off" and stop listening. But this king is also a judge. His throne is also a bar bench, so he has to hear Paul out. His Majesty and His Honor are a captive audience, because they are the guarantors of due process. Paul has a committed ear from this royalty. What a privilege indeed!

So, with the amenities behind him, Paul lets loose with his testimony. He tactfully reminds the judge-king that his faultless manner of life from his youth is well known. He moves on through his adult years of strict observance of the law as a Pharisee. He sees himself accused for believing the promise of God to the fathers. Still framing his case in the tested terms of legalese, yet fashioning it as flowing personal testimony, he goes from his persecution of the saints to his conversion and call. Then he moves in for the kill—the juridical coup. With the king's full and rapt attention, he drives home the punch line: "Wherefore, O King Agrippa, I could not be disobedient to the heavenly vision." It is a great stroke! No wonder he is thanking God under his breath!

Move 3

This seems to be his pattern throughout. Whether we can see what he sees to be thankful for or not, *he* can see it. Perhaps it's because he believes that God works in *every* thing for good (Rom. 8:28). He is strikingly consistent; there's that *every* again. Thanks for him are not just a habit or a courteous gesture for special blessings; thanks are based on a well-thought-out belief system. He has a way of interpreting life in the mood of gratitude.

Listen to the beginning of his letter to the church at Philippi, a few verses after the word about thanking God at his every remembrance of them. He is in jail, and he knows they are worried about him. He says (1:12-14): "I want you to understand, brothers and sisters, that what has happened to me here in Rome has actually brought about the advancement of the gospel. I get to give my witness before the palace guards and everybody else around here. And there are folk who were once very wishy-washy, who, having seen how I take this imprisonment, are much bolder in the faith. So you see, regardless of how and why I preach, the gospel is indeed preached, and I'm real glad about that."

I would have a hard time taking unjust imprisonment the way Paul does, but I can surely join him in rejoicing, given this distance in time and 20/20 hindsight. It dawns on me that Paul writes more of the New Testament than any other single individual, and that this would never have happened without Paul's being under house arrest in Rome. Here he sits, the greatest theological and practical thinker of the early church, with *time to write* only because he is a prisoner. He is a busy, energetic fellow, and he gets around! But God lets him be placed in the relative comfort of a guarded private home of his choice, with visitation rights and mail in and out. There is disgrace, perhaps, in being in custody, or under house arrest. But we are all the richer because he was incarcerated and because the blow did not crush him. He chose rather to *work* during confinement, with his heart, mind, and pen. He was giving thanks in everything, and we are blessed.

Once, many years ago, I heard of the discovery of relics of very early Christian worship in the northern reaches of Germany. There were speculations about how this could be, so soon after Christ. I had and still have a theory about how this happened.

A man named Paul is a house prisoner in Rome, with a different Roman soldier chained to his wrist every day. This fellow writes a lot, but sometimes he gets writer's cramp so he has to find something else to do. He's not much for taking naps and such, so he looks around for some way to use the time. He sees this soldier chained to him. Why not give *him* some of the Word of God? He starts to communicate, and some listen eagerly. But if they don't, he jerks the chain and wakes them up. Some of them find his witness to be life changing, and they seek out his followers in the palace and all over Rome.

These same soldiers who guard Paul get duty all over the Roman Empire. One day one of these soldiers is talking to another in northern Germany. They have been transferred up there to do their temporary time in the hinterlands, like all of the troops at one time or another. This soldier happens to mention a person named Jesus, and the other one is startled. "How did *you* find out about *him?*" he asks in astonishment. The answer comes back, "They put me on guard duty one day in the home of a strange little guy named Paul. When he finished his correspondence, or whatever he was writing, he turned to me and started talking about this man Jesus. I was fascinated, and I wanted to follow him." There are a lot of people on this post who have had the same experience. The word spreads like wildfire. They set up a place of worship; and that's how Christian relics turned up so very early so far from Rome.

Move 4 (Celebration)

God works in *every* thing for good, so we can *thank* God in every thing! The very budget of the Roman Empire, which builds an almost timeless system of roads and aqueducts, can be used for missionary purposes. Those very roads can be used to transport missionaries, and these soldiers can be won to service while they are still soldiers in uniform and on salary. The empire's military budget is God's missionary budget. Hallelujah! I see now how Paul stays so thankful.

I had some terrible chest pains in a pulpit once, and all of a sudden the breath coming out of my mouth was too weak to be heard. We were only a block from an early detection heart center, one of three in the nation at the time. They rushed me to it, and they let me smell the pretty oxygen. They monitored my heartbeat for days. I am alive today because of an adequate but not life-threatening warning. It happened in a perfect place at a perfect time, but I didn't seem to hear Paul as I should have. Paul might have said, "While you're watching that monitor you're not supposed to be able to see, try thanking God. This is no exception to the rule and, besides, thanks will help you heal faster. In *every* thing give thanks!"

On my next attack, they did an angioplasty on my heart. As I lay there watching the cardiologist work, it dawned on me that this man was giving me maybe twenty more years of life. When I was a child I used to laugh at this predictable prayer by Deacon Jackson, but now I was ready to shout it from that cold steel table: "Thou hast lengthened out the prickly thread of our unprofitable lives and bidden our golden moments to roll on. Hallelujah!"

Whatever happens from now on, I'm going to thank God. In *every* thing? Yes! *Every* thing! Whether it's raining or the sun is shining, in good times and in bad, whether I'm popular or in oblivion, God is worthy of *all* my praise and thanksgiving. Let every thing that hath breath praise the Lord! For as long as we have breath, we have something for which to be thankful. "In *every* thing give thanks!"

HERO AND HEROINE TALES

The character sketch can be very effective when used to provide heroes and heroines, especially for the young. Every child needs a collection of familiar favorites. Not only does the preacher "sell" a single sermon's behavioral purpose; at issue is the potential for a collection of traits forming a full-blown human being with whom the preacher and congregation become intimately familiar and formative favorites. Over time, there can be many more, and these Bible characters can become familiar to the hearers by a kind of spiritual contagion, one trait at a time. The preacher has come to feel toward Paul as if they grew up on the same street, in the same block. And the congregation comes to feel the same way. One sketch, then, is part of a series on Peter, if not indeed part of an annual visit or visits with "our friend Peter." Another series on several such heroes and heroines equips both children and adults with crucially formative models.

My own parents thought nothing of using their reserve of biblical personalities for a variety of conversational purposes, for example, "I feel like Moses felt when . . ." Their nonstop identifications made their pastors' sermons much more meaningful to them, to say nothing of the resource such sketches became for us children, and for the pastors themselves, on a cumulative basis.

A CHARACTER-STUDY MODE

There is a mode of Bible study that aids this accumulation. It should be used in all sermon preparation, but it is especially important for character sketches. Instead of reading the Bible in desperation, to seek material for preaching, one reads in a mode of presence. Words are heard and people are seen and related to in the mind's eye on a kind of wonderful wireless television, to be turned on and off at will. Just as sermon hearers are expected to be drawn to personal identification with biblical characters, preachers should develop a warm and intimate relationship with our Lord and with these heroes and heroines. It is this concrete sense of closeness that can be so spiritually contagious and wholesomely influential in the lives of young and old alike.

The Bible is more treasured seen as a living collection of admirable characters, servants of the most high God. This is richer than when it is simply a source of abstract ideas and rules in cold print. One tends to require at least one Bible in every room of the home, for ready reference. But this book is now simply used to enrich our image of our friends in the Word and to verify our spontaneous memory of precious sayings by which we live. It is no longer a proof text for debates or a pool of quotations with which to show off. The book gets worn and the thin sheets torn, but it is treasured too much to be fully replaced. A new Bible was bought, but it was hardly used after a new cover was put on the sixty-year-old personal companion, with all those notes on the pages and all the characters in color that it calls forth from pages in black and white.

The chapter that follows is devoted to the similar sketching of groups of people, as opposed to individuals. Natural groupings by faith and race and class and nationality have their own peculiar characteristics and their own special needs. These too can be reached and helped to become blessings.

CHAPTER 6

Variations on the Group Study

The term *group study* as used here denotes the portrayal of a body of people who have their own cultural, ethnic, national, educational, socioeconomic, religious, or other label. As an identifiable group, regardless of size, they have their own fairly common strengths and weaknesses; problems and accomplishments; causes for concern and causes for celebration. Since all of these labels issue in what could be called a variety of traits, it is clear that this "group study" genre is the plural parallel to the character sketch of individuals, as just studied. The vivid portrayals and identifications in response, and the timing and celebration are similar. The pastor of the congregation is simply guided to speak to their needs as a group, and the congregation tends to respond as a group.

The group study seeks to move whole groups to act or to grow in specific ways. What habit is to a person, tradition may be to a group. The resistance to change can be greater, however, given a group's loyalty to itself and the fierce desire to maintain its pride and solidarity. In a word, the need for sensitivity, tact, and creative diplomacy is greater with group studies than with character sketches.

For instance, a highly unified group of veteran church officers would not be amenable to change-oriented counseling one at a time. As a group, they would be even less amenable to any prophetic (and direct) criticism from the pulpit. After a new pastor's patient endurance of the standard period of orientation and the winning of influence, a sermon of the group-study genre might be appropriate. The group studied would be the group of "officers" helping Paul spread the gospel to the known world. The text might come from his epistle to the first church at Colossi: "These only are my fellowworkers unto the kingdom of God, which have been a comfort unto me" (Col. 4:11b). The lesson in the liturgy might be Romans 16:1-24, which lists twenty-seven of Paul's fellow workers. The b.p. could be to move lay leaders to accept needed changes in the ministry of the church as the body of Christ.

This group study would seek to draw leaders into identification with Paul's huge and laudable staff of friends. With these heroes and heroines the local leaders would adopt Paul's team's gracious manners and their same pattern of cooperative assistance. Special care should be taken and research done to avoid the temptation to sketch Paul rather than to study the group. The challenge to the preacher is so to depict the large, varied "staff" that they draw the admiration of the local hearers, who then identify with and engage in behavior changes toward the habits of these dear colaborers of Paul.

The sermon might be introduced with a graphic bar chart showing rapid decline of traditional churches in America, with commentary in contrast on how the church *first grew* with none of the conveniences we enjoy. Then one might raise the question: How the dickens did Paul do it? The sermon could then begin with a Move I, declaring that Paul didn't do it by himself; he had this huge team of coworkers who did the legwork.

I heard the great Harry Emerson Fosdick do an unforgettable midweek Bible lecture on this huge band of laborers whom Paul mentioned by name. Fosdick marveled at the twenty-seven names in Romans 16 alone, and at the geographic spread, cultural varieties, and unique challenges. Fosdick's b.p. was related to Paul as pastor, for the benefit of us students and future pastors. However, I thought even then (sixty-five years ago) about what a team of beginner laity that must have been, as they were vividly described—and about what a fantastic result they had in reaching the whole of the known world of their day. It is out of the contagion of the preacher's admiring response to the early leadership that he or she wins open ears from today's lay leaders. And, of course, the celebration in such a sermon is about what that early crew meant for the worldwide body of Christ of which we today are a part and by which we are unspeakably blessed.

This opinion on dealing with entrenched traditions and established groups must not be mistaken for mere church politics. I have warned every class I ever taught not to use their influence until they get it. But this homiletical approach to groups is more than that. A group's traditions are what brought them to where they are. Most folkways are treasured for cause and are to be respected. Traditions are not surrendered easily. One virtually never wins in frontal attack on culture, as seen in the Crucifixion itself. But there are times when one is called to choose a cross, even in a pastorate. Let such be chosen, however, in full preparedness to find influence elsewhere.

Group change is undoubtedly in the will of God, but it is better inspired than critically admonished, if one plans to remain a while. Predominantly negative sermons, whether to individuals or to groups, are usually ineffective or worse. Indeed, if a people easily accepts too much use of the pulpit as a whipping post, injury is done to the healthy self-esteem and spiritual wholeness of that congregation or other body. It could be called spiritual masochism. Well-chosen group studies lift up the *prophetically positive* possibilities and common values of a natural community of persons, especially in the celebration of the sermon. This genre harnesses groups to aspirations to ever-greater spiritual maturity and kingdom service as a body.

The examples presented in his chapter demonstrate the various ways in which any model event involving two or more persons, or even a single person symbolizing a group, can be used to motivate and teach another group. The first example presented is transcribed from a sermon by Miles J. Jones to a worshiping congregation gathered to honor a colloquium of prospective writers. The behavioral purpose of this sermon as a whole addressed the self-esteem needs of the congregation as members of an ethnic minority. The section presented here appeared only incidentally to be addressed to the writers honored, while speaking still to the entire group. Naaman's life is the subject of a study of a symbolic group.

The message was based on 2 Kings 5:1-14, the story of the prophet Elisha's healing of the Syrian commander Naaman. The sermon text used was the first verse: "Now Naaman, captain of the host of the king of Syria, was a great man with his master, and honourable, because by him the LORD had given deliverance unto Syria: he was also a mighty man in valour, but he was a leper."

The sermon, under the title "Naaman's Problem and Ours," yielded enhanced motivation for group self-esteem and achievement. There were also relevant insights and sympathetic motivation for dealing with lepers. The audience quickly succumbed to their common bond with the protagonist, a visible characteristic generally perceived as more important than character or competence. The hearers readily identified with this man whose great accomplishments were nullified by the word *but* and the word *leper*, which followed. The word *Black* was never even mentioned until very near the end of the sermon, but the audience's attachment to Naaman was by then complete. The b.p. of self-esteem and motivation for achievement was well accomplished if the response of the hearers was any measure.

An obviously well planned but seemingly casual aside to us, as aspiring authors, was even more significant and memorable.

> Behind that word "but" was that which cancelled out all the rest of his capabilities. But he was a leper. . . . We perceive this person to have some difficulty which we scornfully associate with physical appearance. It negates all else that he or she would be or do. This was Naaman's problem, to be perceived negatively: to have one's contribution in life nullified or negated just because one's understanding of reality is not the same, and because one is perceived as being "less than," and therefore subject to a disregard.
>
> It is important for us to appreciate and understand this, because, you see, another leper did not write this. Had this been written by another leper, "but" would not be there.
>
> "And" he was a leper would be there. A leper's perspective changes the grammar. If lepers were to write this story, it would sound different. But let those who do not suffer the malady of this condemnation write your story and you will always be behind the "but." Your definition will always be behind the conjunction of contravention. "But!" It makes no difference, but . . . It's dangerous to let somebody else write your story. It's dangerous to let somebody else define your existence. We've got to write our story ourselves, if it is to be told properly.
>
> I wonder what it would sound like if lepers had written down Naaman's story. I wonder what kind of compassion would have attended this designation, had lepers written it. I wonder what kind of understanding might have seeped into Naaman's condition of existence had somebody else written the story. It doesn't mean that he wouldn't have submitted himself to the healing waters of the river, but it does mean that the perception about him might have been utterly different. There is this understanding that when one is disadvantaged and disregarded, there is need to have one's own story told by those who understand that condition of existence. And not until that is done, and done with faithfulness, can the true cause of the condition be put before persons.

I found it hard even to imagine a more appropriate way to motivate the work of that guest body of writers. The group identification had been complete on the basis of broad parallels of existence. When this motivational thrust was made, we were completely open to it and moved toward our purposes of being there, with joy and celebration.

The next example of group study focuses on the *family* of Timothy. This is a portion of the sermon devoted to group study. The balance of the sermon offered a set of parallels for families to motivate underprivileged youths to achieve their highest potential by encouraging them to celebrate the resources they already had.

STIR UP THE GIFT (SAMPLE SERMON)

When I call to remembrance the unfeigned faith that is in thee,
which dwelt first in thy grandmother Lois, and thy mother
Eunice; and I am persuaded that in thee also. Wherefore I
put thee in remembrance that thou stir up the gift of God,
which is in thee by the putting on of my hands. For God
hath not given us the spirit of fear; but of power, and of love,
and of a sound mind. (2 Tim. 1:5-7)

In order to get a better grasp of what this text might be saying to us, I invite you to join me in what might be called a case study of the Timothy family. It is like Bible detective work, and the modern parallels of available resources are many and obvious.

Paul mentions Lois and Eunice, Tim's grandma and mom, in glowing terms as model Christians. He calls to remembrance their sincere faith. This is an unparalleled compliment, yet they had not always been in the faith at all. It would appear that as members of the Jewish Diaspora, the dispersion of the Jews beyond Palestine after the fall of Jerusalem, Lois and Eunice had come to be somewhat ashamed of their Jewish heritage. Theirs was a minority race, a minority culture, and a minority religion in Lystra, or wherever they actually took up residence in Asia Minor. So they took names from the prevailing culture, which was Greek. Lois was a *Greek* name, as also was Eunice. Eunice took a Greek husband; no serious Jew would do such a thing. There is every reason to believe that she had no desire to be known or identified as a Jew.

They were "passing" for members of the Greek majority. This identification was so complete that they did not bother to circumcise Timothy, as every true son of the Law surely should have been. He had no such telltale mark of Jewish heritage. We know this because Paul had to have Timothy circumcised before he could expect him to be accepted in the work he sent Tim to do in Corinth.

Of course, the name Timotheus was manifestly Greek. This not only shaped him in the image of a Greek in the eyes of the public; it also pointed him in the Greek direction in terms of self-image. People name their children after what they hope they will be, and one of the most telling clues of our time is the fact that many people no longer give their children biblical names. They go for football stars and movie actresses. I like the Hispanic habit of naming some of their children after Jesus. They are not ashamed of that name. Timothy's name means "one who honors God," but Lois and Eunice were not ready for an Isaiah or a Jacob. Up to the time Tim was born they were still in this mode of identifying into the Gentile majority; they wanted him to think of himself as a Greek.

All we can say from this point is that something world shaking must have happened to Lois and Eunice during Tim's early years. By the time Tim was in his late teens or early twenties, they had established themselves as unashamed Christians.

They were willing to suffer not only as Jews, but also as members of the even more persecuted sect of Jews, namely the Jewish Christians. Thus Timothy had been exposed to the Christian faith throughout his formative years, to such an extent that Paul could say of him that he should be an example to *everybody* in the faith, old and young (1 Tim. 4:12) Paul felt confident in sending Timothy to the hardest church on his missionary circuit, Corinth, because he had grown up in a family that was Christian to the core.

Now, his family heritage was not all Timothy had to offer in the sight of his mentor, Paul. Paul must have been seeing a great advantage in Tim's competence in Greek language and culture. In addition, Tim was just naturally gifted; he was smart. Moreover, he had his own deeply rooted personal faith experienced in the warm manner of his family's deep Hebrew roots. Do you realize what he had? He had the best of *two* worlds—two major cultures and worldviews. Now that's a tremendous combination!

Paul was keenly aware of this because of his own experience. God had subpoenaed him to do this same kind of witnessing to the Greek-speaking Gentiles. The original apostles were largely unlettered speakers of Aramaic, and the gospel had to be bridged out of their insular limitations. When a Hellenist Jew was considered as a replacement for Judas, they passed over this bilingual brother in favor of another person with only Aramaic like themselves (Acts 1:23-26). They blamed the choice on the straws they were drawing, but I have my suspicions. The Christian faith could never be a world-class religion with this parochial bunch.

In effect, God said that since they wouldn't appoint Matthias, the Greek-speaking candidate, for a seat on the board, the best thing to do was arrest one. So, one day on the road to Damascus, God stopped the smartest man available, struck him from his beast, shook him up really good, and blinded him for a while. This is how God acquired the services of the most gifted writer of the New Testament. Paul knew very well that somebody would have to carry the bilingual gospel when he had departed this life.

So Paul told Timothy, the gifted multicultural whiz kid of the early church, that he had no reason to be afraid. God had given him gifts far beyond those of the folk of only one culture and no family faith background. Tim must stir up these gifts, for God had not given "the spirit of fear; but of power, and of love, and of a sound mind" (2 Tim. 1:7).

The final example of group study is taken from a sermon preached for a congregation's "Education Sunday," and is entitled "To Teach Them Diligently." It was directed to *parents* as a group facing the ravages of urbanization, secularization, and attractive materialism among our young. This version of the sermon is a condensation of the theme sermon of the 1978 summer series on NBC's *National Radio Pulpit*.

TO TEACH THEM DILIGENTLY
(SAMPLE SERMON)

These words, which I command thee this day, shall be in thine heart: And thou shalt teach them diligently unto thy children, and shalt talk of them when thou sittest in thine house, and when thou walkest by the way, and when thou liest down, and when thou risest up. (Deut. 6:6-7)

A popular pastime in America today is the lamenting of lost traditions. None is more lamented than the widespread loss of deep faith, which nourished integrity and strength of character in life's storms. Now it may be that this tradition never was so pervasive as folk say it was, but even if it is only nostalgic exaggeration we still need desperately what it affirmed, as a model. So I want to share with you in this series some biblical affirmations that I have believed all of my life, because they still have remarkable power. They got lost from our everyday repertoires because they weren't passed on adequately. Since every life is lived by some kind of religion, formal or informal, in place of the old tradition we have absorbed a "folk" faith dictated by the mass media and oriented to the selling of material things. It's a religion of getting and supposedly enjoying, to the exclusion of almost everything of spiritual and ethical value.

Today we need to get at least equal exposure time in the hearts and minds of our children. This problem of "equal time" is not new. Moses had it in mind when the priests recorded our text. Of course the priests of Moses' day didn't have to compete with television, but the original religion of the wilderness was heavily threatened by the constant exposure of the Hebrew youth to the materially more attractive culture of the Promised Land. Whereas Canaanites enjoyed guaranteed sun and irrigation water, with predictable, healthy food crops, the Hebrew culture had depended on wild game and plants and prayer. The Canaanites were well-nourished and attractive *people*. The young Israelites were bound to see how much better looking their neighbors were. These youths couldn't help hating their own food and fashions.

Look again at these nomads who wore ragged skins for clothing while the Canaanites grew linens and dyed them in elegant patterns. But that's not all; the Canaanites lived in fabulous houses of stone and mortar, with windows set to catch the breeze and built-in stone tubs for cool bathing. Who could ever again appreciate anything associated with living in tents?

The Canaanites had a much more attractive religion, built around agriculture, with a lot of wine (a crop) and dancing. They even had sensuous rites celebrating the increase of their flocks. Hebrews might have won control of the land, but they were losing badly where it counted most: in culture and religion.

As the Hebrews settled into the Promised Land and grew more comfortable, however, the big question became, How would they stay as close to God in this comfort as they had been in the wilderness? The priests advocated a saturation of their consciousness of God's presence, word, and will. Parents were to talk about God at every opportunity, but *casually and naturally in conversation,* in the midst of the flow of life in pleasant ways: "when you are out walking or sitting at the table, when you are going to bed, and when you are getting up." Parents were urged to express their faith and insights in the very verses of the Bible: "these words which I command thee." In a word, they were to be so happily and casually full of their trust and values that every single minute that they were with their young would be a spontaneous teaching moment. You see, the priests realized that the unspoken and subtle things they did were teaching what they really believed even better than what they said formally. And so it is with us today. Parenting hasn't changed much.

The problem is not one of having so much time that we overindoctrinate; it is, rather, a matter of trying to compete with the time and influence that the prevailing culture already has. If we don't use every second, our children won't have a choice. They can't choose a faith they have never encountered, and this world will do its best to see to it that they don't. Parents at most can only manage to keep alive for our children the option of serving God in an abundant life—this in a majority of servants of mammon.

Parents may be overwhelmed by so constant a task, but who is more handily positioned to teach our children? And if the words are, like the text states, *in our hearts,* how can we avoid teaching them every minute of our lives? We only have to spend more time with our children and be more intentional about communication from our hearts.

I have said I was raised in this tradition. I can recall many experiences in which my folk shared their faith in Bible terms. Daddy wasn't very pious, but he taught much good religion on the run. He was a humorist to the end, but the faith in his very bones was always leaking out.

One day we were planting our vegetable garden down by the railroad tracks. At some seven years old, I was busy planting corn, one kernel in each hill. Dad insisted that I put in three or four. "Why?" I wanted to know. "It only takes one." His natural and instant response was, "They that sow sparingly shall reap sparingly" (2 Cor. 9:6). Not all kernels were alive, and good farmers avoided depending on only one. I left a few hills the way I had them and found that Dad was right. Because of the way he handled it, I had no inclination whatsoever to resist it as a biblical authoritarian interruption into my life.

Years later I was a Boy Scout, and Dad was the leader on our first camping trip. Some boys from another troop had regaled us with tales about pranks, and we could hardly wait to get started. I conspired with some friends to plant pepper under the noses of selected persons in the middle of the night. Dad was among the elect. Their sneezing as they awakened was oh so funny! There was only one trouble with pranks; the time came when I was the selected honoree. The trick played on me was so traumatic that I still cannot recall what it was, but I can never forget Dad's response. I ran to him crying, and he had a hearty laugh. Then he waved his finger and declared, "Be not deceived; God is not mocked: for whatsoever a man soweth, that shall he also reap" (Gal. 6:7). The twinkle in his eye told me that he knew who had put that pepper under his nose. And the whole experience taught me not only to remember the Word, but also to understand it with uncommon clarity. Lessons with such real-life audio-visual aids are etched in little boys' souls for life.

That must be why the priests suggested chatting about our faith in the midst of real life, rather than depending primarily on formal class instruction: "[Thou] shalt talk of them when thou sittest in thine house, and when thou walkest by the way, and when thou liest down, and when thou risest up" (Deut. 6:7).

I know this is overkill, but I can't resist telling one more of these stories. It was the year of the great crash on Wall Street, but we had our own tragedy; Dad was sick for three months. As Christmas approached, we three Mitchell brothers had a summit and concluded that Santa Claus didn't apply to us. We were steeled to accept whatever came, and tried to be satisfied that such a good Dad was still alive. We went downstairs Christmas morning, jaws tight, and determined to be little men. We were completely unprepared for what we saw: rather large boxes marked for each us. Our aunt and our new uncle had decided to brighten our day with a pair of roller skates for each one of us. We could hardly contain our joy.

Once again Dad was busy interpreting what was happening in terms of the Bible. But this time he wasn't laughing. With joy in his heart, a tear in his eye, and a big lump in his throat, he declared, "I have been young, and now am old; yet have I not seen the righteous forsaken, nor his seed begging bread" (Ps. 37:25). It was a bit heavy for little boys, but we understood. And I have never had to memorize that verse either. Who could forget it after such an experience?

Praise God for pleasant parents who use any time and place to teach the Word! Thank God for saints who equip youth to face life with irresistibly memorable verses! Praise God for folk who just naturally speak interesting Bible-ese! Those priests were absolutely right: "Talk about it and live it when you are sitting at home and when you are walking to the grocery; when you are getting up in the morning and when you are going to bed at night."

CHAPTER 7

Parables, Metaphors, and Similes

We come now to more of what we have been calling "genres." These, however, consist of a wide assortment of structures, images, and figures of speech, *all* of which are used here for teaching by *parallel*. Concrete things, easily seen and grasped, are used to explain indirectly things that are directly expressible only in the general or abstract. The discussion of technical genres, for example, narrative, metaphor, and simile, however, should include all parabolic meanings. But some of the biblical parables simply will not fit classification as any of these genres. These we will call "parabolic narratives," a separate genre from the simple narratives already discussed, and from the metaphors and similes to be discussed later in this chapter.

PARABOLIC NARRATIVES

For instance, the parable of the rich man and Lazarus (Luke 16:19-31) does not fit the formula for narratives in chapter 4. Which one is the protagonist? Hearers would not normally identify into the situation of either. Yet the hearer is likely to sympathize with the underdog at the beginning and identify with his comfort at the end. The problem is that the b.p. is in the rich man: how *not* to be selfish with one's material possessions. So one tells the story in its usual stages knowing these dynamics. The celebration is easy and instructive, and the b.p. is accomplished by parabolic narration. A lesson in unselfishness is taught, and a behavior is influenced without direct identification with poverty, but with the necessary emotional involvement.

The parable of the laborers cited above is another fairly typical narrative told with parabolic meaning. The guidelines for simple narration do not apply. Again, who is the protagonist? The hirer; isn't his the crucial action? No! Then what is the b.p.? Actually, it isn't in the hirer; it's a lesson in trusting the grace of God, a form of behavior for the hearer. So the story is told, again, in its usual stages; and the hearers rejoice and celebrate God's gracious openness to late believers.

In this parable the hearer is not likely to identify with and try to be like God, but rather to *trust* God. It is obvious, then, that for preaching purposes not all of Jesus' narrative parables were directly behavioral. This is especially true since this laborer parable could be said to have doctrinal or trust purposes. The trusting workers aren't the protagonists, though; the hirer is. Nor is the b.p. of trust exemplified in the hirer. In formulaic terms, the trust simply doesn't come from the usual identification *with* the chief character. Rather, it is directed *toward* the chief character, God. The hearer's belief is the purpose, even though God is implied as protagonist in the mind of Jesus as he taught.

This option, then, becomes an important exception to the narrative formula of hearer identification with the protagonist, who embodies the b.p. The hearer here is moved to trust, nevertheless, and that is the purpose after all. The simple narrative contrasts with this parabolic narrative because it suggests an alternative pattern used by Jesus. Rather than having to fit one's style into a standard narrative definition, this relieves the preacher of any concern to properly match the three elements of narration. It helps to know this, especially when there is more than one option for the choice of purpose and protagonist in a narrative.

In summary, it is obvious that for preaching purposes not all of Jesus' parables were narrative and directly behavioral, especially since these two samples could be said to have what might be called a doctrinal or trust option, which is a less visible form of behavior. Here the trust is not exemplified in the protagonist. In formulaic terms, the trust simply doesn't come from the usual identification *with* the chief character. Rather, it is directed *toward* the chief character, God. It is important to note that this hearer's belief option, with God as protagonist, is no doubt the version in the mind of Jesus as he taught, in both of these parables. These options, then, become important exceptions to the narrative formula of hearer identification with the b.p. through its embodiment in the protagonist. The hearer is moved to trust, however, and that is far more important than conformity to a formula. We move now to an alternative to both simple narratives and parabolic narratives: metaphors.

METAPHORS: THE ISSUE

The word *metaphor* is not used in the Bible, but metaphors are well represented among the parables. Matthew and Mark say that "without a parable spake he [Jesus] not unto them" (Matt. 12:34 and Mark 4:34; Luke reports Jesus' use of parables fourteen different times). The technical name given a parable (whether narrative, metaphor, or simile) is not so important; it's how the words function in the preaching and teaching processes. The fact is that Jesus used them all.

For instance, Jesus used a metaphor, "Ye are the light of the world" (Matt. 5:14), as a figure of speech. But light might also be cast as a participating "person" in an imaginative journey on a winding road. Light then becomes a protagonist or other character in a narrative. In either case, the hearer is motivated to serve as an enlightening influence—a guiding light in a dark world. Thus an abstract principle called light (spiritual insight) is explicated by the concrete image of a lamp or candle.

Modern metaphoric theory confronts us because the value of *metaphors* in generating and communicating meaning is being widely reexamined and explored theologically. These discussions are well worthy of the attention they have drawn in scholarly circles. However, the value of these analyses in week-to-week sermon preparation is considerably less, and further from the primary purpose of most of Jesus' parables. While the rabbis of Jesus' time used parables to win debates on the Law, Jesus used parables to help ordinary laity live the abundant life (John 10:10).

The theological issues, therefore, are treated in the appendix. The rabbinic technical interpretations of Hebrew parables in Jesus' time are mentioned in the appendix also. At this point, suffice it to say that the metaphoric theorists find some agreement with the sermonic exegetes—that Jesus was revealing expanded theological meaning as well as influencing behavior. The difference is that the theorists place much more emphasis on parables as radical innovators of abstract theology. Jesus' usual audiences heard more practical guidance for life and faith.

This difference is clearly seen in the interpretations given to the parable of the laborers and the hours (Matt. 20:1-16). For scholars, this was an exciting break away from theological tradition. For the common people, who heard Jesus gladly (Mark 12:37), it was good news for late converts to the faith, a symbolic narrative parable to help people visualize and fully accept God's grace personally at any age.

This textbook is based on the assumption that Jesus' parables were primarily for simple salvation and spiritual and ethical-moral growth. It is true that Jesus' theological brilliance was manifest in intellectual bouts with Pharisees. The fact remains, however, that the common people did hear him gladly and that Jesus' imagery in metaphors and similes was for the purpose of remaining within their grasp. This would suggest that these common people were Jesus' primary interest and audience.

PARABOLIC FIGURES: NONNARRATIVE METAPHORS

Jesus made wide metaphoric use of parallel *figures*, with no narrative or dramatic action whatsoever. So also do persuasive speakers, sacred and secular, in our time. When political orators speak of an audience as the "salt of the earth," the figure is drawn from Jesus' metaphor in Matthew 5:13. This saying has such common use today as to have a meaning all its own. That meaning, however, always comes from the uses or functions of salt, which haven't changed since Jesus' days on earth.

The spot reference use of figures is relatively simple, but the use of a figure as primary text for a whole sermon is much more complicated. This has been briefly outlined in chapter 2, page 24, where a figure (salt) supplies characteristics, each of which becomes an increment of meaning. These increments are used as major moves in consciousness, which are the main sections once called "points" in a sermon.

The following subfoci or elaborations might be given for each of the major moves:

I. Salt makes eating more pleasant.
   A. Salt makes all food taste better and eating more pleasant. When blood pressure goes up, and we are ordered off of salt, we really miss it.
   B. Our church's ministries combine very pleasant food with pleasant people.
   C. Christian love makes people pleasant to be around and draws people close. Tell story of delinquent child who hung close to pleasant, loving camp counselor.
II. Salt preserves, preventing the forces of decay.
   A. Since time immemorial civilized societies have kept meats from spoiling by "rubbing them down" and saturating them with salt.
   B. Some of us have seen the process in the country on hog-butchering day.
   C. True Christians preserve society. Tell story of Wild West sawmill mission.

III. Salt is supremely fulfilled in complete self-sacrifice.
   A. Salt is consumed in the fulfillment of its purpose. It must leave the shaker.
   B. Salt can't be used again, regardless of use: flavor, preservation, or gargle.
   C. The greatest people are the most self-giving. Tell TV story, *This Is Your Life*.
   D. Celebration of Jesus Christ, who thought death was not robbery: Phil. 2:5-11.

The issue of timing the increments of meaning in the design of this sermon has already been mentioned in chapter 3, page 34. This third treatment of the salt metaphor emphasizes the arrangement of details within the moves. These details support the ascending sequence of emotional intensity and suspense, toward the peak celebration.

THE USE OF SIMILES

The study of metaphors as parables is almost always linked with the study of similes in a similar kind of role. The difference between the two may seem insignificant at first sight, but the very fact that Jesus used both metaphor and simile is sufficient to justify some attention. Whereas a metaphor would say, "Ye *are* the salt of the earth," a simile would say, "Ye are *like* salt."

In his extensive teaching about the kingdom of heaven, Jesus said situations were "likened unto the kingdom of heaven" ten different times. In the parable of the wheat and the tares (Matt. 13:24) "the kingdom of heaven is likened unto a man which sowed good seed in his field." Linguistic analysis would suggest that this is not as strong a statement as the "is" of a metaphor. But "is" would shock the ears of the hearer, because it would be overstatement. Jesus' choices were always appropriate. It is probable that today's preachers make no conscious judgments on this. Possible similes are everywhere.

Many years ago I preached what I thought of as a parable sermon based on the "metaphor" of an automotive engine's cooling system. I realize now that it should have been called a simile, if indeed it is at all necessary to give any *parable* an additional technical name. The words "likened unto" were never applied, but they were implied. The text was Galatians 5:22: "The fruit of the Spirit is . . . longsuffering [i.e., patience]." The occasion was Laymen's Sunday. The major moves were parallels to take care of major parts of an automotive cooling system, such as hose clamps, freeze plugs, thermostats, and radiators.

Intro: Story of raised hoods on cars (all kinds, new and old, large and small) in a desert. Why? One problem in common: inadequately cared for cooling systems.

I. Every automobile engine requires regular disciplined maintenance.
   A. Hose clamps and head gaskets need routine examination and tightening.
   B. Freeze plugs need checking for leaks.
   C. Every Christian needs to start the day in prayer, for spiritual checkups.
II. Every automobile has a thermostat to keep the motor at the proper temperature.
   A. A broken thermostat can misread as too cold and burn up the engine.
   B. A worn-out thermostat can misread as too hot and overcool the engine.
   C. Many mistake friends as enemies and need new spiritual thermostats.
III. Every automobile needs to have its radiator flushed out periodically.
   A. The greatest cause of overheat is foreign matter clogging up the radiator.
   B. The greatest cause of hot temper is the dirt of selfishness clogging up the soul.
   C. The easiest way to get rid of hot temper is to flush the self out.
IV. A good auto mechanic can repair and overhaul the least promising car.
   A. When we saw the hoods up in the desert, our car was a repaired junker.
   B. The mechanic apologized for the looks, but guaranteed the cooling system.
   C. The fruit of an overhauled spirit is longsuffering (patience), and I can celebrate it as a recovering hot-tempered child.

The amazing response to this lay-centered sermon was because of the component of *familiarity*. All real similes should be chosen on the basis of familiarity. Most laymen fancy themselves to be at least shade-tree-level mechanics. This sermon not only spoke in familiar terms; it caused their faith to bless their greasy workplaces and reduced the social distance between pastor and people.

Another such nonnarrative figure with high familiarity used in simile is found in a portion of a sermon preached to seminarians by Nathan Dell of Richmond, Virginia.

SAMPLE SERMON

In this rejoice not, that the spirits are subject unto you; but rather rejoice, because your names are written in heaven.
(Luke 10:20)

When I was a student at Savannah State College, near the end of the final semester the registrar's office would post on a bulletin board in the lobby of the administration building a list of the students who could expect to graduate. You should have seen us crowding around that place, trying to get a glimpse of our names. If your name was not on the board, you would not be allowed to graduate at that June's commencement. If your name was not written there, you could not march with your class. It was not hard to tell the students who did not see their names. They would walk away; some crying; others silent, sad, eyes straight ahead or glued to the floor, too embarrassed to look you in the face.

But then there were those who saw their names on the list. Their gladness would not allow them to keep silent or remain still. There was a shout on their lips, a leap in their legs, and a light on their faces. Their names were written on the graduation rolls!

They went back to their studies invigorated and renewed. They still had to finish clearing up the bills they owed the college, but that was all right now, because their names were written in the "book" of graduation. They still had to attend classes and finish term papers and take final exams. But none of that mattered now; the board in the hallway bore their names.

I wonder if *your* name is written in the registry of the family of heaven? Have you so received the Lord in your life, so trusted and obeyed that your full name is unmistakably inscribed in the Lamb's book of life? Have you so studied and fulfilled your call to preparation that your name is on that list of those both called and obeying? You don't have to receive honors; it's just that if you can say yes, it will make a great difference.

I know it makes a difference with me. Whatever duties remain, I can perform them; my name is written in heaven. Whatever burdens are left, I can carry them with enthusiasm; you see, I have been informed that my name is on the list up there. Whatever difficulties are required, yet to be faced, I can deal with them. My surname and given name both are inscribed in that beautiful book. Life's problems may still be complex, but I can handle the situation with God's help.

I can keep the faith now, even if I can't keep the pace, because my final finish is firm. I can finish this course now, even if I'm sick and can't get well. If my tongue never was very powerful, and even if I lose my speech, I have an inheritance on the books over on the other side, and I'll hold out until I get there. If I have worked no miracles and moved no mountains, and even if I can't move one side of my own body, it's all right. My rejoicing is undimmed and my happiness in the Lord is complete. As Jesus said, "I can indeed rejoice in that my name is written in heaven."

Within the already mentioned limitless supply of figures with possible use as similes, there are many not noticed right in the Bible. The following example is the beginning of a sermon on the manger of Bethlehem, a Christmas sermon. It also doubles in a weeklong series on the spiritual significance of healthy self-esteem.

THE MANGER REVISITED (SAMPLE SERMON)

And she brought forth her firstborn son, and wrapped him in swaddling clothes, and laid him in a manger; because there was no room for them in the inn. (Luke 2:7)

Please come with me to visit the babe at Bethlehem. This time, however, I propose that we do it with some new understandings. For now, at least, let's do away with much of the customary sentimentality. Let's not have any more of this "po' li'l Jesus." I simply cannot justify pity for Jesus, and I'll tell you why in a little bit. But first, let's get off the desk clerk's back. The town is crammed full. Everybody and his brothers and sisters are back home to register with the Roman government. With no prior reservation at the one inn in town, the Bethlehem Holiday, you simply don't have a ghost of a chance of getting a room.

This desk clerk is only doing his job when he finds it impossible to accommodate even a pregnant young woman in labor and nearing delivery. If he didn't have a room, he just didn't have a room. He could lose his job if he tried out of sympathy to take away somebody else's room.

Now I do know from experience that there are exceptions. When I worked at the Deshler Wallick nearly seventy years ago, I would hear every now and then that a wealthy (and important) person had arrived at the desk with no reservation. The alarm would go out and we were ordered to "make a room." At that point we would have to "create a room" in a few minutes. Of course, these folk were regular customers with much money. It was the desk clerk's job to work magic on their behalf. That clerk at the Bethlehem Holiday was not obligated in the least to create an obstetrics ward.

It must not be assumed that this clerk was a cold-hearted fellow; he had no other option about rooms. I know he was caring because he led Mary and Joseph out the door, around the corner, and down to the stable. We've got to stop giving that desk clerk a hard time. He took the risk of keeping Mary on the premises and offering her the best he had.

Having hopefully won some acceptance for the desk clerk, let me add that I have no problem with the stable and the manger. A feedbox differs very little from a cradle, except for maybe a rocker. That hay in it is a form of grass, and it is clean, soft, sweet, and comfortable. When I was a child I walked through fields and pulled stalks of hay and ate the bottom inch. It was sweet and very nourishing; why worry about the hay?

In fact, why worry about the swaddling cloths? Rich or poor, all any baby ever gets is a diaper. There are no high-fashion diapers for babies; have you ever heard of a Brooks Brothers diaper? If in today's world one is offered the choice between paper disposables and soft cotton diapers, I'll take the cotton every time. That's a swaddling cloth. Not only does one not need any more than that; the baby couldn't use it if the baby had it. And the same is true of his menu. Doctors still say that breastfeeding is best.

Like I said, Jesus is not to be pitied. As far as we know, he had five fingers on each hand and five toes on each foot. He had all his mental faculties, two loving parents, and his health. The wise men had no trouble finding him, and neither did the shepherds.

Jesus had everything he really needed. There are no doubt many babies born on this planet who do deserve to be pitied and who are bereft of many necessities. But, the way I see it, Jesus wasn't one of them. There are among us in this congregation babies who didn't do quite as well.

To tell you the truth, I'm fully convinced that the manger was in the very will of God. Quiet as it's kept, there were many, many advantages to this manger birth.

The Savior of the world had to be accessible to *everybody*. There is no problem for a king to come down to visit at the bottom, but there would be great protocol problems if the wretched of the earth sought audience in royal circles in order to pay homage to Jesus. No matter how poor we are, or how we are socially stratified, we can get to Jesus, the child in the manger.

I might add that the manger is also a convenient place for the visitors to get together. "These here shepherds" are right out of the field and they haven't had time or place to bathe or shave. They are dressed for the field and they have been sleeping there for days. I know of no other place where these two groups, royalty and sweaty herdsmen, could find common ground if they should have happened to be there at the same time, which they weren't. The manger had strategic advantages.

Also, there is clarity of perspective that the view from the bottom provides. It's a philosophical advantage; the existentialist philosophers say that if you want to understand a civilization, ask the slave, don't ask the sovereign. There are two reasons for this. One is that the slave is at the bottom, so he can look in an upward direction and see the whole thing. The other is that he has nothing to lose by telling the truth. If the report comes from half way up, there may be privileges to protect. It may truly cost too much to tell the truth if one is at the top. But if a report comes from the bottom, there's nothing left to lose. In the folklore somewhere, slaves were known to have said for the ears of their masters, "I been down so long, down don't bother me." God wanted the Savior of the world to be born in this position of superior wisdom and objectivity.

I keep looking at this manger, and I see God in history, renewing the world's leadership from the most unexpected circumstances. No dynasty or tribe or class of people can maintain a monopoly on high places for very long. God is reminding the powerful people of the earth that they can't automatically pass their superior gifts on to their children unless the Giver empowers it. And any child, no matter how illiterate or debauched the parents, just might be a brilliant future contributor to the welfare of all mankind. Manger children can go all the way to the top, and God guarantees that some do.

Gardner C. Taylor, that prince of preachers, tells one of my favorite stories. He recalls spotting a childhood friend in a large audience one evening many years later.

This friend had grown up in a shack at the far corner of a cotton patch. His parents were poor, illiterate sharecroppers. He had often narrowly escaped being financially forced to leave both college and medical school. His life was sprinkled with deliverance by narrow escapes, but he had never given up. Nor had his God ever failed. At the time of their tearful reunion after the meeting, he was a distinguished heart surgeon and Chief of Cardiology at a great medical school. In this manger child from Louisiana God was manifesting the fact that origins do not finally determine endings. And God the Creator of all the world's intelligence can and does raise up whomsoever God chooses, from mangers and all sorts of other unlikely places.

This hope-giving truth was celebrated in the final move of the sermon, and the preacher added to that rejoicing the fact that he himself was also a manger child, in whose childhood the comforts of electric lighting and central plumbing and heating had not yet arrived. The congregation included many others familiar with manger-level beginnings, and the rejoicing was gloriously contagious.

It is good, then, to know the difference between a metaphor and a simile, and to know when a narrative is a meaningful parable for which it is not necessary to make any further technical distinctions. The Apostle Paul was using a simple metaphor when he wrote, "Now then we *are* ambassadors for Christ" (2 Cor. 5:20). Jesus was clearly using similes when he declared that the kingdom of heaven was *like* a grain of mustard seed, or *like* leaven or yeast (Matt. 13:31-33). Jesus' uses of simile, metaphor, and parabolic narrative were equally effective in the parable of the last judgment (Matt. 25:31-47). The whole scene was introduced with "as," indicating what it was like, simile fashion. The sheep and goats are considered by some to function as metaphors for the people under judgment. But the entire narration is clearly parabolic, although introduced as if it were a literal account. It is good, then, to know and use the first two, and the *parabolic narration* category implies wider latitude for good narrators.

Various Sources and Uses

The choice of so many of Jesus' uses of metaphors and similes should not be understood to exclude or overlook the richness of other biblical sources such as the Apostle Paul, or the "parable possibilities" in ordinary contemporary life. Indeed, the potential sources are limitless. To illustrate this scope of figures, here is offered an outline on Paul's use of ambassadors. Nathan Dell's use of college reports (pp. 81-82) and my own use of the manger (pp. 82-83), as previously presented, also illustrate the range of parabolic figures.

The Apostle Paul's second letter to the Corinthians (5:20) includes this metaphor: "Now then we are *ambassadors* for Christ, as though God did beseech you by us: we pray you in Christ's stead, be ye reconciled to God."

I. My citizenship is in heaven.
    A. This world is not my primary residence.
    B. The home office supplies all my security and sustenance.
    C. My ultimate loyalty is to the kingdom of heaven.
II. The messages I bring are from the home office.
    A. The Word I bring is dictated from the home office.
    B. I am to be received as a representative, more messenger than authority.
    C. My diplomatic portfolio is, "Be ye reconciled to God."

III. My term of office is limited.
A. I am appointed for a stated term only.
B. My labor is urgent.
C. I look forward to retirement to my permanent home.

The Gospel is enriched and empowered by the use of concrete parallels. Jesus' employment of metaphors, similes, and parabolic narratives did not degrade the message in the least. On the contrary, it not only rendered the message reachable to the humble; it elevated it to a quality of inexhaustibility for the learned.

We move on now to a genre heavily dependent on the previous genres. It is called "expository preaching," but it varies from popular tradition in that it focuses on a biblical text with a single theme and behavioral purpose. This contrasts with traditional running expositions on many texts, suggesting many themes. Although the definition proposed here covers less Scripture, it goes deeper in the exposition of what it does cover. Expository preaching as defined here uses other genres to make this single-theme text come alive.

CHAPTER 8

Expository Preaching and the Combination of Genres

It is my strong conviction that all preaching should be exposition of the Bible, in the sense that preaching, by definition, is based on the authority of the Bible. The major purpose of this book is to help preachers bring that Word to life—to experiential encounter. Much of biblical truth is brought to life in the genres described in previous chapters, but much is also expressed in cognitive increments of meaning—abstract principles and doctrines. To bring these to life, one needs vehicles of encounter once again. Thus, biblical exposition and expository preaching are composed of increments of meaning that are brought to life by such things as parables. This is what Jesus did, and we will find that most of our sermons are expository, needing the use of brief stories and metaphors to bring the text and its increments of meaning to vivid experiential encounter.

The outline of every expository sermon, therefore, will reveal a genre made up of genres—a series of increments of meaning, each brought to vividness by a concrete image of parallel insight. This series of insights will flow coherently from the primary text of Scripture, and will be timed in impact to conclude in celebration. Preachers all have different styles, but this fundamental sermon structure and flow will apply to each and every one.

Classification into genres is not vitally important, except to remind preachers that they must know which of several genres and their structures is to prevail. That is, one must establish a firm understanding of which genre controls the sermon outline and places the other genres (the various moves in consciousness) in sequence. It is here that the expository genre comes in handy; no one of the subgenres rules. The controlling principle of organization is in the flow of the various increments of meaning in the *text*. This was illustrated in the chapter 2 exposition on Romans 8:28 (providence). Excerpts follow.

"And we *know* that God works in all things together, for good to them that love God, to them who are called according to God's purpose" (author's translation).

Move I	God works in *every* thing. ("Hairs of your head are all numbered" [Luke 12:7].)
Move II	God *always* works for the good of the called.
Move III	God *always* squeezes good from the most evil of deeds. (Gen. 50:20)
Move IV	We *know* we can trust God's providence. (Celebration)

These moves in consciousness are increments of meaning extrapolated from the abstract text by linguistic analysis. Each move is expressed in a topic sentence and has to be made vivid by a concrete narrative or other genre. In this case, Move III is made to come alive by the story of Joseph and his brothers, with a vivid key subtopic of how Joseph's brothers meant it for evil, but God meant it for good. In Move I, Jesus mentioned sparrows and the hairs on one's head. I added the number of the unswept hairs on the floor of my dormitory room. (Concrete images!)

A variety of genres can be found in most sermons, apart from the primarily expository sermons just discussed. These genres have a way of overlapping and being included inside one another. Of course, there is no reason to call attention to a genre in use in a subtopic, or to a change of genre, except on rare occasions such as: "This reminds me of the story of . . ." In the sermons that follow there are varieties of genres. These are pointed out to illustrate the value and discipline of awareness, as advised for the clarity of focus in sermon design.

In "The Other Women," the basic continuity and primary genre is that of a *narrative*. However, we need to know more of the characters in this story, so this is provided with brief *character sketches*. The basic continuity flows in the minds that made the crucial decisions so uncommon in their culture. Thus there is some *stream of consciousness*. In addition to all of this, there is a sense in which the whole narrative represents a subtle study of women as a group or gender. This could easily be rewritten in the form of a *group study* supporting women's special gifts and earned recognitions. With every subgenre there is the possibility of shift of overall focus to such genre, unless it is structurally subordinated.

In the first draft one need not self-consciously label every element in a sermon. Nevertheless, one ought not go much further without checking to be sure that each element is appropriately supportive of the text and main moves in consciousness, and not tending to have a focus of its own. Such deviations can slip into the outline quite unintentionally, so sermon designers are behooved to be sensitive to all the symbolism and signals that may be flowing through the minds of the hearers.

The inevitability of all these concerns is one more reminder that it is God who gives the increase from all these sincere but highly complicated efforts at planting and watering.

THE OTHER WOMEN (SAMPLE SERMON)

It was Mary Magdalene, and Joanna, and Mary the mother of James, and other women that were with them, which told these things unto the apostles. (Luke 24:10; New Testament lesson: Luke 23:55–24:12)

All of Jesus' followers felt an awful desolation there at Calvary. We don't usually associate it that way, but it was like that feeling that overwhelms the people at the prison gate after they have struggled to stop an execution and failed. You see, the Crucifixion was just that: an execution. Jesus had endured his execution between two thieves. It was a crushing defeat of all that his disciples had hoped for, and they pretty much left the scene to grieve, probably in private. After all, what was there to talk about now?

However, there was a righteous member of the Sanhedrin Council who had dissented from the verdict of death. He even went so far as to risk the censure of his peers by requesting custody of Jesus' remains, in order to follow the Jewish law and bury before sundown. To do this he had to provide his own new burial place, carved out of stone. That involved what amounted to a large donation—a capital gift. He may only have followed Jesus from afar, if at all, but his gracious treatment of Jesus more than justified Luke's report that he was a good and just man.

Now, although the official male disciples had left the cross, there were some women who stuck around. After they saw what was done with the body, they ran home to prepare some spices for the proper embalming of the remains. As soon as it was lawful, early Sunday morning, they came back, not knowing how they would get the stone rolled from in front of the tomb. To their complete amazement, the stone was already rolled away, and when they ran to look in the tomb, Jesus' body was gone. A couple of angels told them that Jesus had risen, just as he had said he would. So these female followers had to run back to town and look up the disciples and tell them that Jesus had risen.

Thus ends the traditional and beautiful story of the first Easter morn. Now let's look at this apparently "harmless" narrative and identify the issues. In the first place, who in the world *are* these women? They must surely belong to *somebody*—male, that is. And how on earth do they get away with wandering around unprotected, which would mean unguarded? Mark (15:41) agrees with Luke (23:49 and 55) that they are Galilean, women who have apparently been following Jesus for some time and at some distance from home, since they are all the way down here at Jerusalem.

Now what in heaven's name are they doing together? Common sense would lead me to suspect that they stay together to protect their reputations. But they may have united even more for their protection as *property* of husbands. This sort of a group is *rare*, so they have to stick together to follow Jesus at all. Their husbands are not Jesus people, and there is no way the culture will let them join the official band of disciples. Indeed, the women's groups we see today are in existence for pretty much the same reasons. A lot of husbands still let it be known that they don't want their wives frequenting coed meetings. And it was only a few decades ago that the need for women's national missionary agencies finally ceased. They united with what we call the "parent" body and were given equal status in governance. But the struggle is far from over.

Now another question sticks out here. Just what is the difference between the sisters whose names are listed and the ones referred to as the "other women"? Of course, that just means that they are other than the named ones, not what it might mean today. But I am intrigued by the possible reasons for knowing and listing some by name and not others.

The first one named is Mary Magdalene. She has already been mentioned, with Joanna and Mary, in chapter 8, verse 2, of Luke's

Gospel. He says there that she has had seven demons cast out of her. Now, putting two and two together, I figure that her gratitude knows no bounds; so she gladly travels to Jesus' places of ministry whenever the "girls," as it were, can manage the trip. It stands to reason that she must have had better than usual income and a husband who was likewise glad that she had been healed. Let me state quite clearly that she is *not* the Mary who had been a harlot, but it would have been all right even if she had been the same person.

Then there is Joanna, the wife of Chuza, Herod's steward. If her husband runs the palace, hiring and firing folk and buying all the provisions, it stands to reason that she is wealthy. She is also quite prominent, and I am inclined to wonder just what Jesus did for her that makes her willing to go to such lengths to follow him. Luke apparently doesn't know either, or he would tell us. In fact, all that he tells us is about her husband, which is just about par for the culture. Many people *still* seem to think a woman has to have a husband to have any identity in the world.

Finally, there is Mary, mother of James the younger, and also of Joses or Joseph (according to Mark). Matthew says she is the mother of Zebedee's children, but in any case, she shares with the other two named ladies the fact that she has enough means to travel and the fact that she is defined by the men in her life: her sons.

That brings us to the question of why only these three are named and the others are not. Off the top of my head, I am guessing that they are local folk, but the Gospel writers all agree that the entire group are Galileans. The best evidence available seems to be Luke 24:1, which says that *they* came bringing spices and the others came with them. That suggests that maybe the named three have more money than the others and can afford the expensive spices to be used for the belated embalming. This figures; even in a male-dominated world, women are given *some* recognition if they control some money. True, they must all have been better off than most folk, just to be able to move about, but there are apparent economic distinctions within the group.

Would you bear with me for one more question? It has to do with Luke. You see, he is usually much more sensitive to the concerns of women and children than are the other writers. Check it out. But here he groups these women without their names in a way never applied to men. Paul may speak of Jesus being seen of Cephas and five hundred brethren (1 Cor. 15:4-6), but Luke *names* men. The only answer would seem to be that even though Luke is more open to women's rightful interests than most men of his day, he is not perfect by any means. He is, to at least some extent, still a creature of his culture.

Now let's get on once again with the story. These Galilean women go all the way with Jesus. When the men have left the dismal scene of apparent defeat, they stay on and watch over the remains of their Lord. It seems the least that they can do. They watch and perhaps help Joseph of Aramathea as he takes the body down, wraps it in linen, and carries it to his new tomb.

But wait! These are *respectable* women, and the touching of the dead is supposed to defile you. High priests are completely forbidden to touch the corpses of even their own daddies! It takes seven whole days to get cleansed after you have touched a dead body. *Ladies* ought not to defile themselves. But they don't hear a word of it. This is their *Lord*, and they couldn't care less about the ritual rules of defilement. This may be even more risky than staying away from home, but so what? They will stick as close as they can for as long as they can. The only reason they don't embalm him this same Friday evening is that darkness is overtaking them. And it is Sabbath. And they haven't even had time to go to the market.

The very first opportunity after that is sunup on the first day of the week, and they are right there at the crack of dawn. They have bought and brought their spices, and they are fully prepared to go to work to see to it that the indignity of a criminal's death is not matched by a denial of the amenities of a dignified burial. Watch them as they make their way, pushing the rule a bit and hiking in the near darkness. Jesus is officially dead, but they can't wait to offer whatever amenities they may be able to offer.

All the while they are wondering how they will roll the stone away, but lookie here! The stone is already moved and the tomb is wide open. They rush in, and, *wow*, nobody! They are about to tear their hair with grief and perplexity when two men in shining garments appear and remind them that the Lord had said it would be like this before they left Galilee. They are quite stunned at first, but suddenly they realize the glory of it all and they rush back to town to tell the disciples. Their joy borders on the unbearable: "He is risen, even as he said!" There has never been, nor will there ever be, any greater joy than this. With or without names in the record, this has to be the most exciting moment and the most important news ever!

As I look back, I have to marvel at the very existence of this group. They are not self-conscious nonconformists or feminist radicals aforetime. They are just women whom Jesus has healed and liberated and on whom he has bestowed respect. Here is this woman whom Jesus has delivered of seven demons now serving as the obvious *leader*. Luke (8:2) says that *all* of them have been cured of *something*. Who knows? One may have had an issue of blood (8:43) and another may have been bent over for eighteen years (13:11). Neither can forget that he touched her and broke all the rules in order to heal and free her and give her hope. They were there because they loved the Lord, and they were quite literally united in Christ.

Their gratitude and human sensitivity would not let them leave the job until it was properly and compassionately completed. There were no "minutes" of the women's society; no budget; no officers; no struggles for power or the prominence of office. Only the love of Christ sprang irrepressibly in their breasts at this point. Yes, the work was supposedly dirty and demeaning in the eyes of their community, but it had to be done. It was disgraceful not to be "properly" buried, so it probably didn't occur to them to worry about "uncleanness." The Kingdom's business requires attitudes like this sometimes.

If we, male or female, shy away from unpleasant, dirty tasks, we can't look for a promotion from our God, who requires us to be "faithful in *little* things." If God sends us to "unclean" addicts and AIDS patients, then that's where the action in God's name begins today. Jesus washed feet and touched lepers and used a substance we call spit.

I am reminded that my own mother had some tales like this to tell. She was a church missionary and social worker during World War I. She served among the people brought to town in cattle cars to work in the armaments factories. They lived as they came, for there were no houses for them. She walked the alleys late at night and changed diapers in converted garages and barns. She did laundry and cooked on makeshift stoves. It was risky for a woman, but she didn't seem to know that at the time. The war ended, and in later years I never heard my home church say a word about what Mama did.

This morning I can't promise you any more headlines than Mama got for her labors. She was one of those "other women," like the ones you find in the Bible. And you, like millions of others, may be one of those other women too. Pastors, deacons, trustees, and others may have to stand trial for the way they have exploited and ignored women in some churches, but faithful work cannot be obliterated. Matthew, Mark, Luke, *and* John had to say *something* about such. You may never get a gavel or a plaque or even a bouquet of flowers or your name in the bulletin, but God knows, and the best records of our time will have to do likewise unto you. What you do for Jesus will in some way "leak out." You see, God exercises the right to squeeze a blessing out of even the worst of injustices after we have done all we can to remove them. You'll never, ever, regret the work you did or miss the recognition too much. Just watch!

I think it is inspired imagination that makes me hear the mind of God, as it were, pondering: "What shall I do for these anonymous benefactors of my only begotten Son? How may I go about saying just a little of how I am pleased by their quiet, loyal ministrations? What kind of spiritual gift would be truly appropriate to persons of such great sensitivity?"

Fortunately, all four Gospels have unanimously answered the question. They say that God must have decided on this wise: "Let them have the quiet honor and glorious joy of being first to tell the news that Christ is risen. Let them be the first to announce the Resurrection. They may not be allowed to preach for many centuries, but they will surely preach the first sermon of the new dispensation." Ladies, the credit is yours, with God's blessing!

I don't know what God will do in Cleveland or Philadelphia or anywhere else, but God is still just, and God still works in mysterious ways. Incidentally, you may be interested to know what God did with Mama. Nobody that I can recall extolled her heroic work in my hometown, but I love to go to the church in Berkeley, California, where she spent her last years. Bulletins report the meeting dates of the "Bertha Mitchell Women's Missionary Circle." I just love to hear one member casually state, "That old lady taught us all we know about missions, and it's only right that we will never, ever, fail to recognize and encourage the quiet ministries we saw in her from time to time."

It was Mary Magdalene and Joanna and Mary the mother of James and all those other women who were with them that told the news to the apostles. And we are compassed about with a host of still other women without name—mothers and grandmothers and wives and sisters and daughters who *still* tell the news and live it out, to the glory of God and the help of us all. Thank God for every last one of them! Praise God for that nameless host and for their valiant ministries! Amen! Amen!

The following transcribed excerpts from "The Providence of God" illustrate the various concrete parallels to the three increments of meaning drawn from Romans 8:28, followed by a celebration of the certainty of these meanings.

The sermon was designed and preached thirty years before the guidelines in this book were formulated, which explains the proposed places where this could be improved. The behavioral purpose is obviously the inspiring of hearers to trust God to bring a blessing out of the worst of injustices and mistreatment.

THE PROVIDENCE OF GOD
(EXCERPTS FROM A SAMPLE SERMON)

And we know that God works all things together for good to them that love God, and are called according to God's purpose.
(Romans 8:28, author's version)

[Introduction: Much too long for a sermon. It "telegraphs the punch" by revealing the outline and reducing the suspense; but it was appropriate in its lecture- and sermon-conference context.]

I don't suppose any of us has ever heard of a doctrinal popularity contest. At least I certainly haven't; because by and large—particularly outside the circles of the seminary—we don't normally or intentionally wax theological. But our various cultures are loaded with theological content, and there is a very real sense in which our most important doctrine is not the theology that we discuss in formal lectures and Sunday school. Rather, it is the "on the hoof" theology that we can find as we watch the servants of God in their daily walks. If one were to do an analysis on a number of communities, one could very well then discover that one of the most popular—and in my opinion *the* most popular—is the doctrine of the providence of God.

There is at the base of the life of most Americans—and certainly the African American culture out of which I have come—the conviction, spoken or unspoken, that life is basically good. We just assume that God is good and that life is well worth living. It can be summed up in the providence of God. The Bible has it in Paul's letter to the Romans (8:28). The religious culture of Africa merged with the culture in this country to distinctively and enthusiastically agree with Paul when he said, "We know that God works in everything for good for them who are called to serve God's purpose" (author's translation).

This text suggests three very simple propositions or moves: (1) God works in everything; (2) God is always at work for good; and (3) even evil deeds against us are included in "everything and always." Nothing is outside God's permission or command. There is no more happenstance, no more luck, no more fate, as sometimes people speak of it. God has guaranteed that there will be meaning in all of life. Whatever the evil choices of men may bring about, God reserves the authority—even in these things—to squeeze out a blessing, as it were.

Move I

This word *everything* is quite literal. We heard it last night as the lecturer mentioned Karl Barth's position. But Barth was not an inventor of ideas at this point. Jesus himself pressed the point that nothing is outside God's providence. Jesus put it, "Are not five sparrows sold for two pennies?" And yet one of them can fall to the earth without God's consent. Indeed, "the very hairs of your head are numbered." And there are few things less consequential than that.

Some years ago, as my wife and I were working on our last degrees, we lived in one of these small—I mean *small*—student cubicles.

From time to time I was moved to clean the place. I always marveled at the amount of hair that I had not plainly seen until I put the broom to work. I realized that there must be a tremendous turnover on my head, and then I had a new respect for what Jesus was hinting at when he said that the very hairs of your head are numbered.

Jesus himself was not revealing new ideas either, for clear back in Psalm 33 the psalmist said: "He beholdeth all the sons of men." All of these details symbolically suggest the tremendous, detailed sort of thing that is part of one's sense of the sovereignty and gracious providence of God.

Move II

Neither was it new to my ancestors that God always works for good. This same concept abounds in African traditional religion. My favorite jawbreaker of a praise name for God is Brekyirihunuade: "He who sees all before and behind." Yoruba culture has a name for God— Omwani—that means the abundant satisfier of our needs. African culture abounds with little—I almost said cute—sayings for describing the providence of God. There are little sayings like: "God is the One who fans the flies for the cow who has no tail"; or: "God is the One who pounds foofoo for the man who has no arms [to hold the pestle]."

I suppose the most beautiful of all proverbs comes from the Gonja of northern Ghana. They have a proverb that says: "God has so fixed it that the leper's sandals break only before the camelfoot bush." Of course, it does require a bit of interpretation. God, this proverb suggests, has allowed us to have leprosy. There is no Pollyanna notion about doing away with all evil because of the providence of God. But it goes on to say that problems are "before the camelfoot bush," which happens to provide the fibers with which the sandals can be mended. In other words, this is a beautiful saying symbolically suggesting that God has so made life good that even our problems have solutions nearby. God has so fixed it that "the leper's sandal breaks only before the camelfoot bush."

This is a part of the very culture on the streets on which I have lived, and all sorts of people who make no claim on the church, and who have no obvious piety, are known to call upon this same kind of basic conviction on which to base their hopes and survival.

I have read twice in *Jet* magazine articles in which Lola Falana has been interviewed. In case you don't know who Lola Falana is, she is one of the most outstanding—and I suppose high-priced—stars in Las Vegas. She lives by a very demanding schedule. Yet both times when she was asked how she managed, she simply said, "God will not let more come on me than I am able to bear." It was said with no pious posturing of any sort. She was simply, but clearly, suggesting that in the world in which she grew up, and in which she still lived with all her riches, she was living out of the certitude of the providence of God.

My colleague, a nationally known therapist, and I are completing a book in which a beginning paragraph recalls a tale picked up from the memoir of a former federal narcotics agent. To avoid exposing his real identity he had been arrested along with all of the dope dealers he had exposed in New Orleans. These included Luke, a major dealer who had never, ever, been arrested before. He had always been very skilled at getting off. His cellmates wondered how he would be able to take the change in his circumstances. They also wondered if their new associate was the one who "turned them all in."

Suddenly, a new prisoner was brought in and the conversation shifted from their suspicions of the agent to the new prisoner, who, strangely, still had his watch and belt. This brought great relief to the agent. The prison precautions against suicide-hanging with belts made a better topic of conversation.

At that point, Luke, who was also something of a respected guru of the dope trade, chimed in calmly with his wisdom: "They don't have to take *my* belt. They could give me a *rope* and I wouldn't hang *my*self." He concluded his pearls with this solemn word: "God never lets more come on you than you can bear."

This was in a jail. He was in obvious jeopardy of some ten to twenty years of confinement. He had gruesome prospects, and yet he faced his first hard time in prison with this virtually culture-wide folk doctrine of trust in providential good.

Moves III and IV (Excerpts)

My ancestors in bondage were known to praise God's providence and to see blessings wrested from the worst of circumstances. One of the marvels of their existence was the fact that insanity and suicide were at such a low ebb. It can all be attributed to a positive worldview—the strong belief that God's providential care made life worth living. They carefully picked out the good things in life, celebrated them, and thus begat trust. This approach is valid for all races and cultures, and especially for Christians.

Many years ago, as a staff member in church extension, I worked with a logger layman up in the redwoods of the Pacific coast in northern California. This man double tithed and was responsible at one point for the complete purchase price of the land and a great deal of the construction costs for a new church in a new community. He was a very, very dedicated man.

One day I was eating dinner at home when the phone rang. This man was excitedly calling to say, "I was up in the woods, and I set a charge under a stump to clear a road, but it didn't go off. I waited, and waited, and waited. Forty-five minutes later I approached it to see what had happened. Just as I got near, it exploded." There was a pause, and then he said, "Both of my eyes were blown out of their sockets and I am blind for life. *What is God doing?*"

What had God done to this man? He was a double tither; a marvelous, dedicated man; a man of deep humility. What do you tell him? Well, I gulped, and not just for swallowing the food I was eating. Then I did what one always has to do: I fell back on one of those firm statements of fixed, secure foundation for faith. I said, "Brother James, I don't have a clue as to what God's doing. But I know how you'd better change your approach to God on the matter. I'd say, 'Lord, I know you're gonna squeeze some good out of this. You didn't plan for it to happen, I'm sure, but you're gonna draw a blessing out of this anyway. I *know* you will. I'm sitting on tenterhooks, because I can't wait to see *how* you're going to manage it. Lord, please let me see the blessing really soon.'"

To my amazement, that seemed to satisfy him. And I suppose that's all there is to satisfy *anybody* who goes through any major tragedy: the unshakable certainty of the providence of God. However, for those of us who do have problems interpreting how God is at work in our lives, I have three suggestions that begin with *L:* God is provident in the **leavings**, the **limits**, and in the **last end**.

God manifests providence in the sort of thing one sees as Satan talks to God, who says, in effect, "You can go this far, but you cannot go beyond this" (Job 1:12). There are certain limits set. Paul suggested it in 1 Corinthians 10:13 when he said: "You have no unique problems. Nothing has befallen you that is not common to humanity. And God can be trusted to limit your tests to what you are able to bear" (author's paraphrase). There is a marvelous gospel song by Roberta Martin, "He Knows Just How Much You Can Bear." God is provident in **the limits**, and none of us dares assume that those limits will be exceeded.

When we tell God, "I can't stand any more of this," we're really offering a threat: "Look, God, I'm gonna go crazy and embarrass you if you don't stop this mess." God is not moved by these kinds of threats, of course. But God does guarantee that things will not go beyond our ability to cope.

God is also provident in the **leavings**. There is a sense in which people who believe in the providence of God tend to say that the glass is half full, whereas some other folk would say it's half empty. Many years ago I went to hear Martin Luther King, Sr., speak at the Ebenezer Baptist Church in Atlanta, Georgia. He was talking about this great idea that his mother had given him. She had told him to always thank God for what's left, because there's always *something* left to praise God for. And it struck me that this was a marvelous piece of theological understanding. There's always something. If you've got enough breath to complain, you've got breath with which to praise God.

About ten years later I returned to hear him again. By this time he had lost his son Martin, his son Adam Daniel, and, of all people, his dear wife, who had been shot at the organ in a Sunday morning service. To my utter amazement, Daddy King was still coping. His theme was: "Always thank God for what's left, for there is always enough left to live abundantly if you will."

God is also provident in the **last end**. Many years ago a famous British evangelist named Charlie Taylor had a famous sermon that he must have preached hundreds of times. It was called "Murder the Ump," a parable on a baseball game. It focused my mind on baseball games, and eventually I preached a sermon in which I said, "This game is fixed." The providence of God is so fixed that no matter how many runs the opponent may seem to get, remember it's only the first and second innings, and God has the power to reverse the whole thing and will! For it is not really all settled until the last man is out in the ninth.

We're playing in the game of life in which no matter how the wicked may flourish as the green tree, God has so fixed it that life will always, ultimately, value the ethics, the idealism, and the faith of those who believe in and trust God's providence. God will be provident in *the last end* and "the kingdoms of this world are become the kingdoms of our Lord, and of his Christ" (Rev. 11:15).

I am reminded, in conclusion, that the providence of God is and always was at the very core of our Judeo-Christian faith. It is essential to mental as well as spiritual health; and trust in the providence of God has given the hope and support by which many have survived oppression. It was true of the African American slaves, and it was true of the Hebrew slaves.

This is precisely the witness of Joseph in the culminating scene in the book of Genesis. Jacob's funeral had been held. They had buried him in Macpela in the family plot. The brothers were returning to Egypt, where they had left their families and flocks. As they journeyed in the slow, tedious manner of the day, they held a solemn conference. They recalled Jacob's advice to them—that they should make a clean breast of it with Joseph, for they knew that Joseph was under no illusions concerning their earlier evil intent. They were gripped indeed by fear, and they sent a message petitioning for an audience. It asked that they somehow might be forgiven and allowed to become Joseph's servants—quite literally.

In their personal audience, they bowed to the floor and said things like, "Brother Joseph, we've done some terrible things. We sold you in envy and bitterness, but you bore it all especially well. You suffered from vicious lies when Potiphar's wife unjustly accused you, and yet you were pleasant and agreeable. You served an undeserved sentence in Pharaoh's prison, but you converted your stretch to a spiritual purpose. Then you made it all the way to Prime Minister, and even that didn't go to your head. You've been a gracious person throughout all of this. When we came here you treated us royally. But, as Daddy said, you did it because you did not want to upset him. Daddy's gone now, and we feel like chickens running before a hawk; it's just a matter of time. *Please* forgive us!"

Joseph had been crying the whole time. He lifted up his eyes and said to his brothers, "I knew your intent, the evil in your hearts, but I see it differently. You meant it to me for evil; the God of providence meant it for good."

There is a cosmic principle that says that God can take anything and everything and work in it for good. So ever since those early days, long before Paul said it, we have known that God works in everything for good. My heart rejoices at the very thought. My ancestors rejoiced despite their suffering. Indeed, our Pilgrim foreparents held fast to this same faith, and *all* of God's children find hope and strength and joy in the providence of God. They shout Hallelujah!!

The controlling genre of the next sermon is a character sketch of David, with brief narrative subgenres. The imaginative narrative of a visit to heaven must not be mistaken as the controlling structure. The behavioral purpose of repentance is manifest at the end, and David embodies it.

A MAN AFTER GOD'S OWN HEART
(SAMPLE SERMON)

Old Testament Readings: 1 Samuel 16:1-13 and (inside the sermon) Psalm 51; New Testament Reading: Acts 13:14-22

Call this a dream—a vision. You name it. It's something that was given to me. I was hanging around the halls of heaven and strolling down the streets of gold. As I wandered around one day I saw this handsome, distinguished man. His face seemed so familiar that I got up my nerve and asked, "Sir, somehow I feel like I know you. Oh yes, aren't you his royal highness, King David?"

He stopped and smiled almost mischievously, as he said, "I certainly am, and who might you be?" I was suddenly flustered, but I managed to say, "I'm Henry Mitchell, from Richmond, Virginia."

David   Oh, I see, and what did you do there?

Henry	I taught preachers. In fact, I hope to break all the rules and go back and teach some more.
D.	Pleased to meet you, indeed.
H.	But I'm *really* pleased to meet *you*, your royal highness.
D.	Wait, just call me David. Around here we don't use titles. Everybody's the same before the Father. No highnesses, doctors, professors, or other titles—just people. So if you don't mind, I'll also just call you Henry.
H.	That's great with me; I've always wished it were that way in our churches. Now, uh, David, that makes it easier for me to ask a question that has been haunting me for years. Do you mind me digging into your personal business?
D.	No, not at all anymore. Just help yourself.
H.	OK, David. How's come you were rated as a man after God's own heart when by law you were a principle accomplice in a cold-blooded murder? And besides, you had a few other pretty heavy offenses, if you don't mind my saying so.
D.	That's perfectly all right. Help yourself. To tell the truth, I'm still a bit surprised myself at that rating Paul gave me at Antioch. To try to explain it would take quite a while, but if you have the time . . .
H.	That's about all I *have* got. Please go on.
D.	Well, to start with, I had no idea that God ever paid me any attention at all until that day they sent for me to come in from the pasture. Then there stood Samuel— that awesome presence! I'll *never* forget that day! I was actually filled with the Spirit of God, and I haven't ever been the same since. From then on I knew I was somebody special, with something very important to do in my life. I was given all this even though I was young and I had never been anywhere or gone to any school or even *seen* a king's court. I *still* look back and wonder about how that anointing affected me.
H.	Is that what gave you the nerve to take on Goliath when nobody else would?

D.	Exactly. I wouldn't have dreamed of such a thing, but the Spirit told me that God had to have *somebody*, and God refused to be mocked. So I just went on out there. And I told them that was why I was there—in the name of the Lord. But even with all that speech, I was really shocked when he fell so fast. Imagine! That great big man! Dead already!
H.	Oh, you were innocent then, and God could use you any way he wanted. In fact, I've always admired the high character you showed in the early years. Even when Saul was doing his best to have you killed, you spared his life. You *had* to be after God's own heart when you seemingly weren't even *tempted* to kill Saul, and you had him right there in your hand! You downright refused to get even. You followed that business Jesus talked about later when he told us to love our enemies. You were so clean-cut and upright when you were younger! But *somewhere* along the way you changed.
D.	Please! Don't say it with such finality. I did do some terrible things later on, but I never, *ever*, changed over completely: I just got weak. Now I'm not making excuses, but once I got to be king it was a lot more complicated than most of you Bible students have any idea of.
H.	I'm sure that's true, but Uriah was *killed!* That must have been an awful lot of complication. (I feel funny calling you David and talking like this.)
D.	Go right on. In fact, if you manage to go back to earth, it'll be good that you dug into this and I leveled with you. You're not the only one wondering about that business of my being a man after God's own heart.
H.	Thanks! You always were a big-hearted sort of person. But now tell me about those complications.
D.	Well, to start with, you have to face the fact that it took *two* of us to get into that mess. Yes, Bathsheba was very beautiful, but she was also very ambitious. Do you remember how anxious she was for her son Solomon to succeed me? Well, she didn't just get that way when he

was older. She was that way from the start, and her folk probably encouraged her. Now, mind you, I didn't fight the feeling, and of *course* I wasn't blind to the political advantages of an alliance with her clan. So that doesn't get me off the hook, but she was *not* taken by violence. Do you understand?

H. I'm afraid I don't. Do you mean she was willing?

D. Not only willing, but eager. That whole affair worked out just as that very beautiful lady had in mind.

H. What?

D. Yes, it was no accident that she bathed in clear sight of the place where I walked at night. And she knew just how hard it would be for me to resist the temptation she put out there. Can you imagine yourself a king, able to have whatever, and nobody to challenge you? No police, no news reporters, no supreme court. You are the court. One of the closest things in *your* experience would be slave masters. I can *look* at you and tell that *some* master just couldn't resist violating your great-grandmother. And you understand, he didn't *have* to resist! He was *master!* There was nobody, not even his wife, with the power to stop him. It's a lot harder to be pure when you're a king or a master. *Most* people never have to face such powerful enticements.

H. Wow! I begin to get the drift. That's heavy!

D. And let me share with you another small complication. The only reason I sent Uriah to death myself was that he wouldn't take a hint and be weak enough to stay a night with his wife. If he had, a military court would have sentenced him to death and I wouldn't have had to touch it. As it was, I *had* to have him die for his country; for if he had lived and this business had spread around, not only I as king, but also the country itself would have been destroyed. Nobody else had *ever* brought Israel and Judah together, and nobody else ever got them back together once they divided under Solomon. He *did* in fact have to die for his country.

H.   But wait! Back up, please! You mean Bathsheba was aware that Uriah had to be sacrificed somehow?

D.   That's just what I mean. How could her father have a grandson who was a king if she were married to dear old Uriah? But don't get me wrong. This does not get me off the hook. As I said, it's just a complication that may help you understand that this whole affair wasn't so strange after all. *Anybody* could get started in such a chain of events and wind up a murderer just like me.

H.   You know, David, I kinda hate to admit it, but I guess you're right. Now let's get back to the man after God's own heart. You may not be the cold-blooded murderer I wondered about, but that still doesn't put you as high as after God's own heart.

D.   You won't get any argument out of me there, Henry, but God used Paul to write more books of the Bible than any other single writer, and Paul was a chief accomplice in a murder, just like me. God works with people as they are. And, too, maybe you should look for a moment at a few of the things I did *right*, besides just refusing to kill God's anointed, old King Saul.

H.   Well, everybody knows you were a strong supporter of the temple and the priesthood. Solomon may have *built* the temple, but *you* did all the real preparation. Nobody can take that from you.

D.   And I seriously tried to do God's will *most* of the time. It may not have seemed so to the man on the street, but I constantly sought the guidance of God in making decisions. I didn't just write it in songs. When I sang phrases like "lead me in the way everlasting" or "lamp unto my feet and light unto my pathway," I meant it. I would *never* have been able to govern that huge kingdom without God's guidance—me, a shepherd boy with nothing like formal education! *God* showed me where to look for good ideas.

H.   I can see that, but I must admit, I had never thought of it before. The Bible stories make you look like some sort of superman. Most of us Bible students don't associate

	the spiritually minded author and singer of the Psalms with the war hero, rolling them into one human being.
D.	I guess that's typical. But let me go on to the bottom line of this "man after God's own heart." I know now that the most important thing I ever did was the way I responded to the pointed finger of the prophet Nathan. All else would have been lost if I had tried to stonewall that one. When he said, "Thou art the man," I nearly died. I had *never* felt that bad in all my life. I fell prostrate before the Lord and fasted and cried. Oh, it was an *awful* feeling. And then when the child died, I hardly knew if I wanted to keep living myself. That's when I got the inspiration for that prayer-hymn, or psalm, as you might call it.
H.	You mean the Fifty-first Psalm?
D.	Yes, I believe that *is* what you folk call it.
H.	I sure would love to hear you sing your own song. My, my, my! That would be a *real* blessing!
D.	Well, no, not quite. You see, the original music was for a different language, and the music itself was quite different from anything you could relate to. The best way for you to hear it is from your *own* lips and your *own* heart, praying for your *own* forgiveness.
H.	I can see now why God loved you so, and you *were* a "man after God's own heart." I can't help feeling very close to you myself—close enough to do just what you said and pray *your* prayer and mean every word of it. Mind if I get on my knees like I do when I pray for real?

Have mercy upon *me*, O God, according to thy loving-kindness:
  according unto the multitude of thy tender mercies blot out my
transgressions.
Wash me thoroughly from *mine* iniquity,
  and cleanse me from my sin.
For I acknowledge my transgressions:
  and my sin is ever before me. . . .
Purge me with hyssop, and I shall be clean:
  wash me, and I shall be whiter than snow. . . .

Create in me a clean heart, O God;
  and renew a right spirit within me.
Cast me not away from thy presence;
  and take not thy Holy Spirit from me.
Restore unto me the joy of thy salvation;
  and uphold me with thy free spirit.
Then will I teach transgressors thy ways;
  and sinners shall be converted unto thee. . . .
O Lord, open thou my lips;
  and my mouth shall shew forth thy praise.
For thou desirest not sacrifice; else would I give it:
  thou delightest not in burnt offering.
The sacrifices of God are a broken spirit:
  a broken and a contrite heart, O God, thou wilt not despise.
O thank you, Lord, thank you! Amen! Amen!

We move now to chapter 9, on the last of the genres, the stream of consciousness. It is perhaps strange and new to most preachers, but worthy of serious spot considerations in the contemporary quest for the renewal of the American pulpit. In fact, it is the most "alive" of all the genres.

CHAPTER 9

The Stream of Consciousness

This chapter deals with the genre called "stream of consciousness," as illustrated by the celebration ending the sermon just presented in chapter 8. In this case, this genre consisted of a prayerful reading of selected verses from the Fifty-first Psalm. Its position as celebration in the sermon results from the fact that the preacher identified into the feelings and thoughts of the psalmist. The cry of the psalmist became the cry of the preacher, as adapted to the present by the verses chosen and sequenced.

The rendition exemplified here was limited in length, but it could have been creatively elaborated for a preferably longer celebration. And, of course, the use of the stream of consciousness does not have to be limited to celebrations, nor does the stream always need to be drawn from the Psalms. I have never heard or used stream of consciousness for a whole sermon; such expanded use seems limited to whole psalms. However, the range of other possible uses is quite broad.

In every use of stream of consciousness, the preacher is impersonating or reporting a character who is thinking (complaining), meditating (seeking guidance), or praying out loud. The capacity to communicate very deep feeling is greatly enhanced by this genre. This is illustrated clearly in Jesus' cry of feeling forsaken as he sings or quotes Psalm 22:1 from the cross. Features such as the tone of voice, facial features, and body language increase the power of the words. What might have been an ordinary monologue of petition becomes a powerful experiential encounter with the plea of a real person. Any character sketch can be enriched by a comparable passage of stream of consciousness from the protagonist; and this vivid mode of bringing a character to life is applicable also to the characters in narratives.

I heard recently a "clip," from the inner thoughts of the characters in the account of the son who was healed of blindness and challenged by the Pharisees. It was very entertaining, but it was very enlightening also—and unforgettable. I can still see the parents with their hands in the air and the facial expressions of wide-eyed ignorance as they thought how to avoid responsibility and risk the ire of the Pharisees (John 9:22). I had even preached from that passage, but the stream of their consciousness registered in my memory as nothing before.

Like all powerful instruments, stream of consciousness needs guidelines for its use. The first would be to restrict the use of this genre to the purposes of vivid exegesis. That is, avoid the temptation to employ creative imagination for entertainment (self-conscious comedy), rather than for making the word come alive. The opposite of "entertaining" is "boring," not "informing." So there is a need to entertain or engage the hearers and hold their interest and attention. But we can dare to claim the help of the Holy Spirit only if our motives are indeed spiritual and not self-glorifying.

A second guideline is the need for remaining in character long enough to establish it, rather than bounce around between characters in a show of talent. A clip can easily be too long, but it can also be too short. Hearers need a brief time simply to identify the person in character, if this has not already been done. One then needs a bit more of time to identify *with* that person in the flow.

A third guideline hardly requires inclusion here: stay always in good taste. The outward signs of the inward flow of consciousness are essential, but they are best when done with restraint such as will avoid overkill. The goal is the vivid communication of the whole passage in context, and not an isolated character as an end in itself.

Among items of stream of consciousness that I have included in sermons are poems, some of which are written as having been in someone's thinking. An example is an excerpt taken from James Weldon Johnson's "The Creation."

> He looked on His world
> With all its living things,
> And God said, "I'm lonely still."
> Then God sat down
> On the side of a hill where He could think;
> By a deep, wide river He sat down;
> With His head in His hands,
> God thought and thought,
> Till He thought, "I'll make me a man!"

Whatever the choices made in the concerns thus far, it must be understood that preaching in this genre is immeasurably more than a mere performance. Although all preaching can be said to have some relationship to performance, requiring a character to get into one or more roles, preaching is spiritually far more in depth than good acting.

The Psalms run the gamut of human emotion. This should be true also of any other basis on which stream of consciousness preaching might be done. It is certainly true of the Fifty-first Psalm quoted above: cry for mercy, confession of sin, plea for cleansing and forgiveness, cry for renewal of spirit, plea for joy, promise to teach sinners, and commitment to sing high praises. These types are found throughout the Psalms. The one major type not found in Psalm 51 is bitter complaint. This is found at its peak in Psalm 22:1: "My God, my God, why hast thou forsaken me?" In this psalm there is missing the confession of sin, which may be why Jesus sang it on the cross, expressing the crowning example of the testing of his humanity. This frees us to cry in complaint, completing the gamut.

The emotions of sorrow and joy require expression, as stated in chapter 3. The necessity for "letting out" both involves not only the fulfillment of the emotion; it also involves healing. Healing ministries call it "catharsis." This genre of preaching may be the most emotional of all, and also the most healing, even for our Savior on the cross. In the ethnic culture in which I was reared, this would also be true. Without any label for the genre, I have seen untold numbers of people freed in spirit and healed of massive depression by being drawn into a stream of candid consciousness in a context of emotional support for release.

These emancipated feelings have a critically important place in congregational worship—in singing and in prayer as well as sermons. Indeed, it may well be that deep feelings will be welcomed into middle-class worship more easily than into the pulpit. In any case, that welcome could be the means by which mainline Christianity in this country can be saved.

Before the approach to the details of sermon design in the genre, it could be helpful to note the cultural parallels to this highly significant and healing stream of consciousness. We start with a fairly common though not rigid sequence of feelings, as found in the African American spirituals as well as the Psalms—and, in fact, the blues.

The *first* and cathartic component is bitter complaint, as best illustrated in Psalm 22. The value is to get the burden up and out. But the minute you release the charge of God's abandonment, you are moved to realize that this is ridiculous and you bow in awe of the righteous God. But that's OK. You got it out. The spiritual parallels are lines such as "Sometimes I feel like a motherless child, a long way from home" or

"Nobody knows the trouble I've seen; nobody knows my sorrow." The blues make frequent reference to being blue and having hard times, losing lovers, and being treated "wrong."

The stream of the Psalms flows on from abundant complaint to awe and wonder before God (51:1), to confession (51:3), recollection of historic deliverance (22:4), promise of service (22:22), and promise of praise (22:25 and 51:15). These promises of praise are the *second* or *positive* component for this healing sequence of folk expression.

The spiritual sang on to comfort: "[But I'm a] true believer, a long way from home." Again, they sang on positive comfort: "Nobody knows the trouble I've seen; nobody knows but Jesus. Glory Hallelujah!" The concluding positive of the blues was: "I won't be blue always. The sun's gonna shine in my back door some day." Any stream of consciousness sermon should follow this general outline.

It is probable that every stream of consciousness sermon should be addressed to the discouraged and distressed. In the same vein, the behavioral purpose (b.p.) should be to empower hearers to overcome depression and rise up in spiritual strength. There ought to be no embarrassment about being validated by the healing sciences. The Bible and its Psalms did catharsis long before there was psychiatry, and there is still far more practice in the folk realm than in the halls of science. In addition, there is far more healing hope in the cycle of the Psalms than in anything else on earth.

This concludes the consideration of the genres, vehicles of experience. We move now to the concluding discussion of details such as sermon titles and introductions.

PART III

CONCLUDING CONCERNS

The chief homiletic concerns of this book are to be found in parts I and II. Part III concerns the titles to be given the experiential encounters (sermons) and the titles to assign that work with the encounters. In addition, there may be a whole new style of preaching needing introduction. Worshipers tend to get accustomed not only to the liturgical sequences and special places to sit; but also with a preacher's homiletical habits.

Chapters 10 and 11 deal with the processes of the introduction of what, for some at least, might be the cultural changes proposed here, with all their subtleties and potential complications. Usually one does not lightly move from Western patterns of primarily cognitive worship, which have been venerated for centuries, to a holistic encounter. Its richness, even though inclusive of serious thought, tends to be threatening. Preaching pastors are obliged to deal with these resisters where they are, not where one wishes they were. The opposition has to be fully accepted, even loved, before one engages in well-planned strategies of painless acculturation to encounters.

Chapter 11 deals with concluding concerns regarding the ultimate awe and wonder of true preaching, as a gift from God, the Holy Spirit. After all of a preacher's efforts to offer excellence in the pulpit, the sermon will be spiritually futile without the inexplicable spark that comes only from the aid of the Holy Spirit.

As author, I am compelled to say the same thing about this book. Thus I offer it in awesome gratitude that I was blessed to complete this print phase, and in the humble hope that the Spirit will bring fruitful acceptance of it in seminary classes of homiletics and in pastors' studies, where preparation is made to communicate the good news.

CHAPTER 10

The Details of Title and Introduction

Sermon *titles* are purposely presented here in the last section, because that is where titles belong. All too often have I heard students excited about a clever title when they had not a clue as to what such a sermon might contain or what it might accomplish in the spiritual life of the hearers, or even what the text might be. Titles need to be written *after* a sermon is well outlined, when one can tell what sort of name would be appropriate to this particular message. It is like the naming of a child only after we know if it is a boy or a girl and whom the child resembles.

One needs to be clear as to the real purpose of titles, in addition to differentiating them from other sermons. They are means of attracting souls who might otherwise never have attended. Nonmembers as well as members might not have attended on a given Sunday morning except that a title in the newspaper or on the outdoor bulletin board stirred their interest.

The preacher needs to be very candid about this match between message and title to avoid disappointing seekers. Once hearers have developed expectations, the church's integrity is at stake. The title must be chosen, then, in the full awareness that it amounts to a kind of promissory contract with the public.

Good titles serve also the purposes of a good handle, a fitting and easy means of reference. One often remembers a sermon by its title. A title may actually be the reason the whole of a sermon is retained in memory. The following guidelines may be helpful in the development of sermon titles.

1. Avoid the choice of titles for cleverness, lest the sermon promote the preacher instead of calling forth a memorable encounter with God and the Word. Wherever possible, choose a portion of the text for the title, helping people remember both Bible passage and sermon. A

phrase from a great hymn can serve the same purpose in a title. The focus of a worship service may be greatly enhanced when such a phrase and hymn are employed as closing hymn and invitational. When members hum such a beloved hymn all week long, the sermon and its title are being recalled also.

As I write, I have had just such an experience with the hymn "Come, Ye Disconsolate." And I can't stop singing in my mind phrases from Isaiah 43:2, heard as a hymn more than sixty years ago: "When through the deep waters I call thee to go . . ." It was from the third stanza of "How Firm a Foundation," and the sermon title was "Deep Water Faith."

Examples of other titles drawn from the sermon text, or from a hymn:

"A Charge to Keep": 1 Corinthians 4:2
"To Whom Shall We Go?": John 6:68
"A Drink of Water from Home": 1 Chronicles 11:17

2. Titles need to be no more than five or six words long in order to be memorable. Brevity aids memory, and familiarity helps too. John 3:16 is very familiar, and a title like "God So Loved" or "That They Might Be Saved" would benefit from the common recall.

3. Determine sermon titles as early as possible in order to make maximum use of them in publicity. The appeal is more effective among nonmembers than among members.

4. Refer to the title in the preaching of the sermon to help recall and encourage reference in later conversation.

Introductions to sermons are important though necessarily brief. They determine whether or not the sermon will draw attention. Like titles, they should be developed *after* the main body of the sermon is written. This assures that the audience will hear what has been introduced, rather than have to wonder "where this came from" after a clever irrelevance has been unloaded. The first concern, then, is to be sure to draw attention to the issue of the sermon.

The second concern is to be sure not to settle the issue or answer the question raised. It is important to stay in familiar territory to encourage the acceptance of the invitation to think. But if the answer is already given, the suspense so essential to rapt attention is lost. People's minds wander off to the dinner on the stove or some other topic. The final resolution of the issue needs to be reserved for the last move, where it can be fittingly celebrated.

A third concern is the distinction between introducing the sermon and, with a new audience, introducing the preacher. This practice is necessary even when the preacher is world-renowned. The hearers may be eager to hear whatever this great preacher has to say, but this speaker may need a few words to arrive at a feeling of basic comfort and a sense of rapport. The preacher just needs to signal the shift from the personal introduction, however accomplished, and the introduction of the Word.

A fourth introductory concern is the observance of criteria for brevity: usually no more than five sentences before the announcement of the text. Exceptions prevail when sermons are *expected* to be lengthy (thirty minutes or more), and when no introduction is needed, such as when a preacher is known to tell stories well and simply starts off inside a story sermon.

And now to the awesome concerns of the Holy Spirit in preaching.

CHAPTER 11

The Holy Spirit and Experiential Encounter

A recurrent student concern in my classes through the years has been the need to place this detailed approach to homiletic design in spiritual dimensions and theological perspective. Many have believed that it is not the prerogative of the preacher to have anything to do with understanding how the Holy Spirit might use a sermon to reach the heart of a hearer. Yet that hasn't kept students from trying their very best, on their own, to assure that the Spirit is manifested. They simply want to be able to *say* that the spirit took possession. They sincerely feel, at times, that learning about it in a class will destroy the mystery and put the teacher or the textbook in the holy place where only the Spirit belongs. Many want all the help they can get, but they need a way to fit it into their development of personal doctrines of *how* God guides and directs the preaching event.

These students' needs are not unique; no servant of God, in the pulpit or out, dares avoid the inevitable assumptions on which a whole life's vocation is based. It is all the more important when the spiritual welfare of others may hang on those assumptions. In this book there are not only theological assumptions but also several psychological assumptions that are very important to this approach to the communication and adequate hearing of the Word. If, as Paul suggests (Rom. 10:14), hearing is crucial to saving faith, considerable theological reflection is needed to clarify the role of the human preacher's efforts and technical artistic insight in so awesomely important an encounter. The preacher's task is to provide a *total experience* of the gospel. This is set over against an exclusively cognitive or intellectual grasp of divine truth. The experience-based gospel proposed here is to stimulate the growth of gut-level trust in God by providing vicarious involvements in the encounters where faith has been caught and taught. In the terms of transactional psychology, it means being used by God to stimulate the recording over of the intuitive "tapes" of unbelief with new "recordings" of profound trust in God. This message to the intuitive consciousness (where faith is stored) should be affirmed by the emotive *celebration* of the gospel truth. This gives ecstatic reinforcement to the comprehension of and dependence on the Word of God. Scholarly support for this interpretation of the ultimately unspeakable process is growing.

Recent psychological understandings and artistic techniques need to be discerned in proper relationship to the work of the Holy Spirit. At best, the preacher is only an instrument in the hands of God, who saves all the souls that are saved, and who stimulates living faith using catalysts called preachers, guided by the Holy Spirit.

Notwithstanding, many students have risen to ask if this recording over is a new kind of determinism or divine predestination, with election based on the preacher's skills. They have suspected a kind of behaviorism, void of human will: "So what place does the choice and initiative of the hearer have in this whole process?" Still others have asked for the relationship between salvation and healing, and the place, if any, of sin. If, then, some readers are to give wholehearted attention to the mechanics and technique already addressed here, some of these honest questions will have to be examined and answered.

The first clarification of relationships perhaps best deals with salvation. This is often thought of as first in the goals for the preaching of the gospel, followed by healing, growth, and empowerment. Salvation is all the more demanding of attention because, unlike the other three, it is so much less amenable to any sort of verification or to the tracing of influences on behavior. The purveyors of pat plans of salvation go entirely too far when they purport to speak for God about who is or is not saved, and exactly how or by what spoken formula. Although the "Assurance of Pardon" is an orthodox and patently valid element of traditional liturgy, it is not to be confused with an individual assurance of salvation based on a glib repetition of a man-made prayer or confession. Equally repugnant would be any remote suggestion that there is a cause-and-effect relationship between the efforts of the preacher, as a learned and compassionate healer, and the salvation of the hearer. Whatever the sensitivity and psychological expertise of the preacher, we are all saved by *grace* through faith (Eph. 2:8), and *no* person will know exactly who else is in that number until the final arrival on the "other side." There will of course be those whose gracious manner and glowing spirit will mark them as prime suspects for salvation. They may even have been greatly influenced by some practitioner of preaching who follows the rules suggested here. But there will always be enough folk who appear saved without such ministries, and enough who have heard such to no effect, to keep the greatest artists and healers in the pulpit humble. It will always be God who saves and to whom the glory will be due. Therefore, we human beings must pray, prepare, and preach *as if* the whole responsibility is God's, no matter how useful our best efforts may appear to be. As Paul put it, we must plant and water, but God is the one who gives the increase (1 Cor. 3:6-8). Some years' crops are bounteous; some are not. And the chief atmospheric causes are in the hands of God.

This figure, however, opens up windows of practical insight. Salvation and the visible *fruits* of wholeness are closely associated. Jesus talked as if the saved tree should show forth spiritual health and growth, together with fruitful empowerment for work and witness (Matt. 7:16, 20). Although in the last analysis this too is in the hands of God the Holy Spirit, there is a sense in which the effectiveness of the homiletical "cultivation" of the trees is subject to some dependable mode of evaluation. One doesn't have to take part in the American preoccupation with numbers and supposed success to be sensitive to the growing presence or absence of the fruits of the Spirit among one's hearers (Gal. 5:22-23). The use of a dedicated mind and the openness of a spirit to *the* Spirit can, thus, be expected to yield conditions that appear best to be used by God for the wholeness and growth of persons. One can accumulate awareness of climates in which the Holy Spirit works best and blesses most. Souls and psyches are hard to separate, and the knowledge of the latter may at times be used by the Holy Spirit to gain access to the former.

However, like all figures, that of the fruit tree breaks down if pushed too far. The best weather for crops can be so carefully calculated that the vintners in California's San Joaquin Valley can know exactly how many very hot nights in a summer are necessary for the proper sugar content in the raisins. But it is not thus with the harvest of souls. Even given a certain atmospheric condition, the yield itself is still in the hands of God.

If one were to change the figure to a more crude parallel in baseball, this truth would be lifted up more accurately. Although players practice hitting for hours, and although the managers know well that a .350-average hitter is always a better basis for the hope of a score, no given hitter can be *sure* of hitting at any given turn at bat. Whether there will be a hit, and for how many bases, is never within the power of human beings accurately to predict. There is no exact cause-and-effect relation between the hitter's effort and the result of any given stand at the plate. Success in any one given "at bat" is beyond any human's precise prediction.

Nonetheless, every batting coach knows that for certain hitters certain stances, grips, and swings are more productive than others. The percentages over time reflect the value of good coaching as well as the genius of the hitter. So it is with the preacher who has followed or will follow the kinds of insight offered here. The glory for the saving and healing and help of the hearers goes to God, but God, by the Holy Spirit, uses the truths of many academic and theological disciplines to fulfill the divine purpose. Indeed, the God of all truth is the author and revealer of all these professional means of reaching and serving human need.

This could raise another challenge emanating from a fractious student or two every decade or so: How dare a professor assume that there is such a discipline as homiletics and that any mere human can teach another to preach? The professors commonly assume that what they preach is by the Holy Spirit and between them and God alone. It is outright effrontery to God for a professor to insist on involving a whole class in the preparation of students' actual sermons to be preached in the professors' pulpits. And this in a required course yet!

In the sense that salvation is of God, they are right, since one does not instruct the Holy Spirit how to act in either hearer or student preacher. Teachers and classes, however, *can* offer suggestions where clearly needed. This is with the understanding that the Holy Spirit must finally validate those suggestions if they are to be used in the actual delivery of a given sermon and in future sermons.

To move the figure back to farming, even though Paul fully recognized that it was God alone who gave the increase, or the harvest of saved souls (1 Cor. 3:6), there had to be some planting and watering. It takes training to be a good farmer, even to plant and water. These skills are teachable to open minds. The indispensable value of teaching efforts and books like this is that of making preachers better nourishers of the saving and growth of the human spirit. Although it is all too obvious that books can go only so far, it is also essential that preachers be sure to go *that* far—to ask God to intervene only after they have done all they can do. God *expects* the farmhands of the Spirit to exhaust their human resources at their proper distance from the planted seed before they look to God to cause that seed to move from death to life.

Once again, however, the figure can be pushed too far. Students have just cause to raise the issue of the place of human will or volition; seeds have no conscious will. However one resolves the issue of the roles of Holy Spirit and preacher, there is yet the role of the hearer to be considered. Is there not a danger that this idea of overrecording the hearer's intuitive tapes will be seen as a passive and even involuntary experience for the hearer? The answers come from both Scripture and clinic. Jesus required "clients" to take some part in the healing. One had to get his own mud and another had to pick up his bed and walk. No healing at the clinic or the church can take place without the cooperation of the person in need. He or she must come to the clinic in the first place. It is necessary then for the hearer to cooperate in the whole process and to have openness to and confidence in the healer. Seeds come back to life, so to speak, but souls always keep at least a tiny spark of the image of God in which they were made. That irremovable residue, no matter how small, must be mobilized in the saving and healing process. To believe otherwise is to paralyze both pastor and parishioner, since pastors do not normally share the Holy Spirit's power to resurrect the dead.

What has been said in the clinical setting must also be said of the event called preaching: No soul is saved or blessed when not seeking or at least willing somehow to receive the blessing. Even Paul on the Damascus road was trying to please God, albeit in gross error. People simply cannot be mesmerized into wholeness and a holy life that they refuse to accept. Whether in Alcoholics Anonymous or elsewhere, one has to somehow acknowledge need and express desire. The sermon-generated experience of a gospel truth in some depth has to be *accepted* by the hearer, for recording on her or his own intuitive tapes. One has the option to reject. Although, of course, it is true that one preacher may make acceptance far more attractive than another can, no preacher can by violence break into the intimate space of the hearer's intuitive "data bank" or "disk storage case." No communicator of the gospel can force-record faith over the older "tapes" of fear and disbelief found there. It has to be freely accepted.

It is here that the place of sin in this whole scheme or process requires treatment. There are, of course, tendencies to reject the gospel, which may be traceable to trauma in early childhood or to bitter experience in churches, even in adult life. There is a bottom line, however, where the hearer has to accept accountability for the choices made within the spiritual options seen to be open at the time.

Ezekiel's fresh insight (18:4) delivered to the exiles in Babylon still prevails: One cannot blame parents or anyone else. The soul of the father *and* the soul of the son belong to God. And whichever of them makes the sinful choice, *that's* the one who will die for it. Parents are responsible for what they do with and to and for their children, but they only plant. The response to all influences is ultimately chargeable to the responder. Yes, Virginia, there is such a thing as sin, the willful refusal to seek, hear, and do the will of God regardless of the charisma of those who present that will. No generation can bear responsibility for what any other sinfully chooses, but it must carry its own load. And for the preacher that includes responsibility for acquiring all the skill possible with which to communicate the gospel. After that, as God told Ezekiel, the matter of whether people hear is up to them (Ezek. 3:11).

In summary, the preacher offers, to those who have ears to hear and hearts to heed, vicarious experience of the gospel, here referred to as "designed to be recorded on intuitive tapes." Positive responses on the part of the hearers are so essential that there can be no real preaching without them. Thus preacher and hearer are engaged in a kind of dialogue, whether audible or inaudible, and nowhere is the Protestant doctrine of the priesthood of all believers more apparent.

Now a final theological question underlies and flows out of all this discussion: What sort of innate nature is assumed to be in these persons to whom the gospel is preached? It has been hinted at as a tiny spark of the image of God already, but the question requires more detailed treatment. How far does one have to depart from orthodoxy to engage in the design of these experiential encounters with the gospel truth? Biblical answers range all the way from Paul's confessional implications of total depravity (Rom. 7:12-14) to the Genesis declarations that God made humans in the divine image (1:26) and that everything God made is good (1:31).

M. Scott Peck, a current combiner of psychiatry and religion and author of the best-selling *People of the Lie*, has reluctantly confirmed the existence of at least some rare humans who are so evil as to strike a kind of terror in the heart of the therapist (pp. 64-65). Goodhearted veteran pastors everywhere have encountered at least one or two persons whose demonic behavior irrefutably validates the existence of sin and evil in human beings. For the pastor, regardless of theological training and tradition, these people compel one to maintain some sort of doctrine of sin, even original sin. The suspicion, then, that this book's experiential approach to worship is based on naive optimism about human nature, would be ill founded.

As I have stated, however, a hard and fast predestinarian view would leave no room for a preacher or healer of any kind to be meaningfully engaged in the gospel. Jesus implies by his word to the penitent thief on the cross that no healer has the right to give up on anybody who is still breathing and conscious. This obligation would hold, even though there might be good reason for a pastor-healer to refer a given person or patient to someone else. There is always *some* potential for hearing in every soul to whom the gospel is sent, and that includes the whole world. The estimates of the "wheat and tares" in any given group will vary, but there has to be an assumption on the part of the preacher that there are in every audience those for whom "it doth not yet appear what [they] shall be" (1 John 3:2) in terms of spiritual growth.

A preacher following this experience-centered approach must labor endlessly, in the hope that what looks like a tare is actually wheat. That preacher, however, must be prepared to bear the final sight of the opposite, or the maximum appearance of defeat. In both cases, whether one is accustomed to reaching many and casting out the demonic or not, the matter is finally in higher hands. Thus the methodology proposed here is compatible with all traditional doctrines of man save the extreme opposites of humanism on the one hand and total depravity on the other.

There is elaborated here a preaching methodology that proposes to remove only the first veil of mystery concerning how the Word acts to save, heal, and empower people. It explains how, to some degree, trust or belief may come from the Holy Spirit's use of the vicarious experience provided in the sermon. This uncovering or demythologizing of the first or surface phase of the once-thought-almost-magic impact of the Word, however, only renders the next phases of human response all the more awesome and clothed in mystery. It will always be a miracle of grace that despite the limitations of our best efforts, people are saved and healed and made whole. So it is still altogether appropriate, as one ponders the process, to exclaim with a preacher named Paul (Rom. 11:33): "O the depth of the riches both of the wisdom and knowledge of God! How unsearchable are his judgments, and his ways past fully finding out!"

This chapter 11, then, is only on the threshold of what it is hoped will be a lifelong and joyous growth experience in the offering of the preacher's best, to be used by the Holy Spirit in ways past finding out.

This concludes the main body of this work on describing the process of designing sermons as experiential encounters with the Word. In addition, this last chapter has dealt with how the human labor of design relates ultimately to the work of the Holy Spirit in preaching. For those with further concerns for theological and psychological rationales of the whole experiential approach to preaching, the appendix that follows is offered with joy. It is all too seldom that the awesome harmony between Christian doctrine and clinical psychology is appreciated and employed in the saving and healing of souls.

APPENDIX

A Biblical and Psycho-spiritual Rationale for Preaching as Experiential Encounter with the Word

And thou shalt love the Lord thy God with all thy heart, and with all thy soul, and with all thy mind, and with all thy strength: this is the first commandment. (Mark 12:30; cf. Matt. 22:37 and Luke 10:27)

Jesus' words above, about loving God, summarize the first Commandment. They give unquestionable evidence of a deep concern in Hebrew tradition for the *holistic* commitment of persons to and in the faith. Such a commitment was seen as the very will of God. To confuse detached, "objective" reasoning with authentic "faith" was unthinkable to the Hebrew mind-set. The word here translated "mind" is from a vocabulary that never really differentiated functions within personality. This cultural frame of reference recognized nothing short of the whole human being at all times. Even without stipulating heart and soul and strength, the word *mind (dianoia)* in the text would have included understanding, feeling, and desiring—most of the conceivable facets or functions of human psyches.

Yet, despite this clarity of biblical position, Western culture has for centuries preached primarily to the cognitive or mental faculties, emphasizing the appeal to reason, to the virtual exclusion of other gifts. Today, many writers in the field of homiletics are confessing as much. But it is very difficult to break free of the captivity of culture.

No matter how much they may affirm sermon impact on the "heart," typical preparation has yet to be directed to the feelings. That is, professionally recognized training tends to prepare preachers to address the mental faculties. Period. In fact, there is great need for much new insight about preaching that addresses the totality of human beings in a manner consistent with Jesus' affirmative and holistic summary in the first Commandment. This was the task in homiletic method that was attempted in this revised edition of *Celebration & Experience in Preaching*, as well as in the first edition.

The difference between the two is that the rationale behind the proposed homiletic process is at the beginning in the first edition. In this revised edition, the design of sermons is placed at the very beginning of the book, with the rationales moved here to the appendix. It is no less important, but it allows those seeking homiletic guidance to find it at the outset.

Patterns of sermon preparation in America's cultural mainstream suggest little awareness of the issue of preaching to the whole person. Even less is the awareness of a need for holistic goals and methods. Two simple facts may help one perceive how true this is. One is the reality that primary concern is given to cogency; typical sermon outlines are devised on the basis of largely logical and cognitive criteria.

The other fact is that the very creeds traditionally included in Christian liturgy were similarly designed; their original goal was to answer abstract theological questions in a manner that appealed to reason. The goal was to provide a basis for unity in great empires and ecclesiastical bodies. The point is that this confession of faith was focused on issues almost completely irrelevant to existential concerns and spiritual wholeness.

Preaching to the whole person demands holistic goals and content, and methods that affect all sectors of human consciousness. These are prerequisite if one's efforts are to be used by the Holy Spirit to plant faith in the deepest and most complete sense.

THE HOLISTIC FAITH WE PREACH

The departures from tradition proposed here require at the outset a redefinition of faith itself. The faith assumed to be the goal of the preaching advocated is, like the text, holistic. That is, all of the hearer's heart, soul, mind and strength is to be involved in the sermon event, in order to beget or nourish a faith that involves the entire person. In the temptation experience, Jesus is recorded (Matt. 4:4) as quoting Deuteronomy 8:3: "It is written, Man shall not live by bread alone, but by every word that proceedeth out of the mouth of God." Although human beings need bread, Jesus is voicing the certain truth that ultimate existence is based on the very Word of God. This preached word, then, is literally to be lived by in every facet of human existence.

A common understanding of such a statement would probably be something like a set of rules by which one lives, but Jesus here is speaking of the very sustenance of life. Jesus would surely not deny the need for rules, but this Word is lived by, in the sense that it is lived *on;* life depends on it. For Satan this response means that Jesus' integrity and wholeness as a person, his being itself, is based on the Word. One survives and copes and orders life by means of the very utterances of God to the people of God.

The minute one sees the preached word in these dimensions, it becomes apparent that the Word has to be heard in a manner that reconstitutes one's whole mode of being. The preacher's goal is to be used of God to move the hearers' supporting core beliefs, and entire style of living, closer and closer to the new person in Christ. This will include information and reasoning, of course, but the main goal is not informational; it is, rather, experiential. It is related to the intuitive depths of being, where trust and distrust reside. The faith referred to here is a "gut" faith, with or without the believer's ability to put it into a coherent abstract faith statement, and one lives by it.

Such faith is perhaps best manifested not verbally, but in the believer's comparatively calm behavior under stress. Persons who do not have such core trust suffer holistically, because peptic ulcers, high blood pressure, and other infirmities are often the result of high levels of stress and anxiety. The person blessed to possess holistic faith does everything in his or her power to solve a given problem. After that, this believer just assumes that God will do whatever else is needed. This believer knows that God understands the predicament and has the power and the providential intent to squeeze a good end out of it all. (*Anxiety* is another word for the inability to trust—the gut level fear that God is *not* dependable.) Healthy trust does not have to be called up by efforts initiated in the midst of the crisis; it is already there in core belief. This trust has been nurtured from holistic experiential encounters with the Word, and it resides in the very viscera or "guts" of the believer.

A trust such as this becomes the foundation for all other aspects of the Christian's life and work. One can seek first the kingdom of God with much greater ease when one trusts God so fully. The value system of the Sermon on the Mount is not feared as a great invitation to undue risk. Likewise, the call of Christ to the costly, prophetic reshaping of churches and other human institutions is more gladly undertaken in trust. A person at peace more effectively accomplishes it. In other words, the priestly effort to propagate a holistic faith is not to be mistaken for individualistic escapism or social irresponsibility. It is actual empowerment for the greatest challenges the Kingdom has to offer a seriously practicing Christian. Indeed, the call of God to service can best be heard and obeyed by in-depth believers. Others must struggle much harder to avoid healthfully the pitfalls of surface conformity, putting on a front. They obey God's will fearlessly and without fanfare.

A GROWING REORIENTATION

This brings to mind a glaring oversight many of us have "discovered" only recently: such a faith as this is not begotten by human reasoning, nor does it reside in the cognitive regions of the brain—rational consciousness. Modern researchers are saying that it resides in the intuitive region, that great, right-brain storehouse, whose ideas have not been entered into the human data bank by rational criteria and processes. One must add that faith also resides in the emotions. If fear is an emotion, then so is its opposite, trust. In other words, if one's faith has no emotive dimension and involvement, it is cold and without depth. But more of this later. The point to be emphasized here is that sane faith must be born in a reasonable encounter, but it is *not* born of rational argument. Nor does it reside primarily in the spheres of the mind where logic is the dominant function.

This I should have learned during my teen years. It was then, as I first grappled with intellectual questions, that I was exposed to the Apostle Paul's parallel insight (originally offered, of course, in a context of encouragement to endurers of suffering): "For we are saved by hope: but hope for what is seen is not hope: for what a man sees, why would he hope for it?" (Rom. 8:24, author's version). The power to verify things rationally is a form of "sight," which automatically removes the matter from the realm of faith.

David Roberts at Union Theological Seminary told us the same thing in a philosophy of religion class. He equipped us to defend ourselves against logical positivists and other devotees of scientific verifiability— the idolatry that insists that *all* truth can be measured and proved in a lab. He advised, "Just ask them *how* they know the truth of the assumptions underlying their system of thought. Don't accept the defensive role; put *them* on the defensive. You see, their basic position is one of faith and not sight, just like yours." It worked! Assumptions are just that, because they can't be proved. I have had marvelous success by taking the offensive, just as he advised. But it took many years for me to see what this appraisal of reason meant in terms of the focus of effort in sermon preparation. If I couldn't use pure reason to argue a logical positivist into faith, then why should I expect that reason, from the pulpit or elsewhere, to beget faith in anybody else?

Come to think of it, this is a good thing. Suppose faith were a function of reason, and salvation a response to established data or truth (cf. Pannenberg below); then the ordinary and less than ordinary IQ would be at a distinct disadvantage. To say nothing of the questions all of this would raise concerning the justice of God. Some of the choicest saints I knew in the pastorate were not supposedly well endowed with intellect. Their speech may have been assumed to betray a poverty of thought, but their lives as a whole spoke most eloquently of their true system of core beliefs. We more ordinarily gifted folk can rejoice that faith is not restricted to those who can grasp X number of abstract theories and propositions.

Fred Craddock puts it this way: "Long after a man's head has consented to the preacher's idea, the old images may still hang in the heart. . . . The longest trip a person takes is that from head to heart" (*Authority*, p. 78). The faith on which people bet their very lives comes *not* because one has heard and understood a great flow of logical persuasion, though the love of God demands that we understand all we can. Rather, it is the fruit of holistic encounter with familiar images, whatever one's intelligence level.

Nevertheless, the idea that reason as such has some sort of content, and that faith in some sense is *born* of reason ("sight"), dies hard. No less a serious and highly respected theologian than Wolfhart Pannenberg writes that "believing trust cannot be separated from the trusting person's belief in the truth of the thing in which he trusts and towards which his trust is directed" (*Creed*, p. 6). In his laudable crusade to free the Christian faith from "subjective tastes," which have no "universally binding power," he declares the purpose of theology to be the giving of a "rational account of the truth of faith" (*Basic*, p. 53). He softens this a bit elsewhere when he says: "It is true that in order to be faith in the full sense of the word, faith does not need to be conscious of these reasons in every case, and above all not in their ultimate clarity and form. It is sufficient that the decision of faith actually rests on reasons that will hold up" (*Theology*, p. 271). Many believers still consider themselves looking to reason to produce, rather than to process, the tenets of faith, all of which are beyond either proof or disproof. As Augustine argued, one has to believe first, in order to have knowledge. The very worldview (or vision of reality) that provides the frame of reference within which we know anything at all is *a priori*—a matter of faith, not sight.

THE ROLE OF REASON

Lest it appear that I am completely ruling out rational concerns in the preaching event, let me quickly provide clarity about the indispensable role of human reason. Every sermon must make *sense*. It must be manifestly reasonable and generally consistent with an orderly understanding of God's creation and our experience in it. If a sermon doesn't match mind and Bible, the part of the sound mind that *monitors* such things will shut down the acceptance of the message. Monitoring is a vital function. Without it people are not only vulnerable to nonsense; they are no longer sane.

However, although reason shuts out nonsense and opens the gates of intuition to the true Word, it does *not* itself *beget faith*. Therefore, when one has drawn up a sound outline and coherent flowchart of sermon ideas, one has only begun the preparation. One has assured that the flow will not be hampered by embarrassing contradictions. The demanding task of leading people to faith and then nourishing it remains. One has yet to address the practical issues of human experience, as sensed by intuition and emotion (of which much more will be said later), where faith is generated and retained.

Related to the rational processes as monitors is the responsibility for clearing away intellectual obstacles to faith. The book of Hebrews quite soundly declares that people seeking God must first believe that God is (11:6). For a thinking Christian to arrive at this starting place of God's existence requires, initially, that honest questions be given adequate answers. One dare not open the door of deep consciousness to this nonrational process of faith until one has either a good answer to vital questions or a sound awareness that this is the type of question to be answered only in eternity. It is never healthy to bypass this questioning function arbitrarily.

"Only believe!" cannot be sound advice unless these obstacles have been dealt with. Those who love God with all their minds express that love by seeking reasonable answers to genuine questions, wherever possible, instead of overworking the essential blindness of faith. Faith is genuine when engaged in after reaching human limits.

Of course, people can think they know more and need less than they actually do. For instance, the illusion of autonomous or independent reason has to be cleared away. This frame of reference includes the erroneous idea that intelligence can begin as a blank slate and generate its own content. Appropriate use of reason forces us to face the unyielding limits of the human mind. This opens the way to simple faith.

Reason has many other functions to perform in connection with faith; it is never absent. The very formulation of faith into a statement capable of being communicated and understood requires language. Words are a tool of rational expression. Belief becomes rationally expressed the minute it is shared with any other person. Indeed, even personal reflection and prayer requires this same component of language. Faith is not reason, but it can never be shared, talked of, or even thought about without a reasonable sequence of words calling forth a flow of images and related ideas.

Then there is the whole function of keeping one's faith *coherent*, free of self-contradiction. This suggests the orderly reflection about God, labeled *theology*. But it is not for "theologians" only; it is a necessity for all believers. Peter (who needed Silas to do his writing for him) urged all Christians to be able to give a reasonable or coherent report of their hope (1 Pet. 3:15) to anyone who might ask. One cannot argue folk into belief; but all witnesses bear the obligation to establish the internal coherence and intellectual integrity of their personal testimony. This includes the rational cogency of the system of one's core beliefs, and the style of life that the witnesses have built upon their unprovable but all-important assumptions of faith.

Two other functions of reason come to mind in connection with belief. One is that of motivator in the listening process. Every sermon needs a carefully chosen introduction, designed to raise compelling questions and whet the hearer's curiosity or appetite for truth. Narratives and related genres also create a *suspense* that causes hearers to maintain attention and take careful note of all that is recounted. This suspense is essentially rational, but it impels one to remain emotionally involved and to enter holistically into the deeper realms of meaningful experience. Intellectual curiosity both leads to the fountain of faith and helps the hearer drink experientially.

The other function of reason has to do with the application of faith to the life of the hearer and to all of life. Sermons are expected to help hearers apply the affirmations of their faith to needs in the real world. The book of James suggests that faith without works is dead (2:20). Except for the extreme rarity of a miracle, working faith is irrevocably committed to the logic of the workaday world. Works born of the deepest trust still have to be planned and executed quite rationally for the most part, and sermons have to be written with this in mind.

These six functions of reason are vitally important. They apply before, during, and after a faith-begetting experience in which the heart is strangely warmed. The soul meets Christ on a basis beyond but not contradictory of reason.

It is time now to turn to how faith is begotten.

THE BEGETTING OF FAITH: INTUITIVE CONSCIOUSNESS

No amount of isolated or pure reason can cause belief to happen. Reason may make straight the highway or prepare the path, but God the Holy Spirit brings faith to us through the *intuitive* and *emotive* sectors of consciousness. How, then, does one affect the intuitive and emotive regions of human personality, given the six indispensably supportive functions of rationality? The intuitive realm is affected more directly by *experiential* encounter. Hunches come from we know not where; and "where" is human intuition.

The "tapes" of intuition contain impressions gathered and stored during the flow of life. This input is not examined, adopted, or organized in a *consciously* rational manner. It includes a wide variety of insights from culture, family, church, school and community, and individual experience. The intuitive realm includes such things as taste for foods, responses to varieties of people, and the way one views the world—one's belief system. Intuition can be guilty of harboring prejudice, but it may also contain most if not all of our highest and most valid values and insights. Indeed, its wisdom is quite frequently superior to that of rational consciousness.

In *Intuition and Ego States*, psychiatrist Eric Berne reported on intuited predictions of the responses of inductees made during the essentially intuitive examinations (of forty to ninety seconds) for World War II. They were surprisingly accurate. Other tests of accuracy showed a rate of 55 percent on speedy hunches and 14 percent when the certified professionals had the time to be deliberate (pp. 7-10). In effect, Berne was saying that psychiatrists who employed spontaneous hunches based on body signals and other subtle data were more often correct than those using complicated, consciously rational criteria. All of us, including psychiatrists, make many correct decisions intuitively. We live our lives daily from this database or rational pool of wisdom. The fact that at least much of this storehouse is verifiably sound, and that all faith is in this category, argues for much greater concern among preachers about how to help persons improve these intuitive "tapes" and their habitual responses to particular circumstances.

There is an account in Mark (9:16-29) that illustrates this understanding of intuition and how it relates to belief. When Jesus probed the faith of the demented boy's father, the father replied tearfully, "Lord, I believe; help thou mine unbelief." He was implying that if he had not given intellectual assent to Jesus' power, he would never have brought his son there in the first place. However, he still had a knot in the pit of his stomach, and his intuitive consciousness wasn't convinced at all. He needed help in the place where the real faith is stored. "Help thou mine *un*belief." And this is where most people need the greatest assistance. Even those who have used reason to remove great intellectual obstacles to faith still need this kind of ministry. Rational screening certifies only that it is safe to open the door, as it were, to the room in consciousness where the intuitive tapes are kept. One's principal location of belief and unbelief is inside this deep chamber of intuition and beyond the direct reach of logical communication or reasoning.

It should not be surprising, then, to find that in the providence of God, the Spirit should use this intuitive channel for communication in the receipt and nourishment of faith. Here one can take no personal credit for processing effectively the affirmations of faith and living in trust; the glory belongs to God. Intelligence test scores are not relevant, since faith comes not by rational accomplishment. It is required only that one love God with *all* one's mind, whatever the IQ.

The question then arises regarding what means of communication can reach the intuitive consciousness of a wide variety of intelligence quotients at the same time. What methods are best used by God to "overrecord" or replace the tapes of childhood terrors and distrust, and otherwise strengthen the tapes of trust? The answer, as already stated, is still experiential encounter, but what does this mean?

The term *experiential encounter* is used here to denote a homiletical plan in which the aim is to offer direct or vicarious encounters with and experiences of truths already fully certified as biblical, coherent, and relevant to need. Sermons are reasonable and relevant sequences of biblical affirmations planted in or offered to the intuitive consciousness of hearers by way of what might be called homiletical coworkers (preachers) with the Spirit. This work is done by means of an assortment of rhetorical vehicles, or literary genres, which stimulate the hearer to identify with and take part in these very meaningful experiences. One is helped personally or vicariously to enter the spiritual-theological dynamics of an *encounter* with the Godhead, or a fellowship with biblical or other historical or current characters, and the miracle of faith takes place.

The fact that we can attempt to describe it all by metaphoric use of such terms as *tapes* or *disks* does not diminish the miracle one whit. We preachers simply have a better idea of how to talk about where we think God is working, and how. (By all means, let us avoid the erroneous impression that this is in any way related to behaviorist psychology.) These insights only make the sermons more useful and the preacher a better instrument in the hand of God. The intuitive impact of experiential encounter is a very important part of the resources by which God moves to create the miracle of faith.

Another resource used of God is emotive consciousness, which will be addressed in the section following. This sector of consciousness also can be greatly influenced by rhetorical vehicles and literary genres, and emotive expression can make them even more effective. Fred Craddock says that "the presence of a full set of emotions is no evidence of the absence of intelligence. . . . Effective preaching reflects the minister's open receptivity to those life scenes which are noticeably emotional in flavor but which constituted memorable and important stations along the way most people travel" (*Authority*, p. 85). The place of intuition and emotion in preaching is discussed in chapters 2 and 3.

THE BEGETTING OF FAITH: EMOTIVE CONSCIOUSNESS

There exists a widespread, often unconscious, and rigid opposition to rejoicing in the presence of God as an act of true adoration. The conscious and unconscious restraints of the preacher-liturgist are contagious. Thus the pastor dare not complain that the congregation simply does not loosen up, when the main source of inhibition in worship may well be in the pulpit. We need, then, to develop an understanding of these restraints before we can devise a strategy for breaking them down—to generate what might be called an analytical rationale for this *un*analytical phenomenon called emotion in worship. This is especially necessary in the light of the significance here placed on sermonic celebration.

The Apostle Paul implied that three of the greatest things in life were faith, hope, and love (1 Cor. 13:13), each of them heavily involving *emotions*. This gives preaching a set of goals that inescapably includes those questionable human feelings so long and seriously shied away from. To avoid them is to miss the most important and powerful aspects of human personality.

Expressive or emotional celebration should be understood as *thoroughly biblical*. The Deuteronomic admonition is one of many: "And ye shall rejoice before the LORD your God" (12:12). Many of the most significant and moving passages in the Bible are characterized by praise and celebration. Few Christians are probably aware of just how *un*biblical it is to be as solemn and stern as most worshipers in Western culture tend to feel is proper.

The traditional use of the word *celebration* in connection with the mass of the Roman Catholic Church is indicative of a historical association of worship with emotional rejoicing. Again, the shorter catechism of the Presbyterian churches plainly states that the chief end of humankind is to glorify and *enjoy* God forever. Yet the worship of virtually every mainline denomination is severely inhibited emotionally. Even now, as these words are read, there likely are residues of sincere resistance to any serious practice of authentic, emotional celebration. This is discussed in chapter 11.

I do not speak as an outsider, because I have often reacted according to very Western expectations. Some years ago I visited an Ethiopian Orthodox church in Addis Ababa. There I saw "debtura" (somewhere between deacons and clergy) dancing with great dignity beside the sanctuary. Their flowing robes and huge drum made an impressive spectacle, but my first impulse was to view it as a bit silly. It took a little time for me to become sensitive to the fact that this type of worship was in the category to which *all* Christians should relate easily. In fact, in the debtura's efforts to follow David and the Bible literally, the real complaint could have been that they were actually too *discreet*.

It disturbed me that I, a product of African American culture, should be inhibited about joining with those debtura. I enthusiastically affirm authentic shouting; I fully consider it a blessing. But though I accept and rejoice in this much more dramatic form of celebration, the idea of those dignified, robed elders dancing before God found in my unconscious depths some irrational resistance. This despite the fact that dancing is so important in African American culture, and that it is so acceptable in theory.

The experience of this one person illustrates the penetration of Western dualism among educated Americans generally. Any dancing, especially among nineteenth-century Protestants, was an activity of the "evil flesh," rather than an art form. To break out of this cultural straitjacket it is important to visualize and understand that these inhibitions are opposed to the very will of God.

A more detailed look at the cultural roots of these inhibitions may also help. Their origins are in an ancient Greek dualism of flesh and spirit. Some four centuries before Christ, a group called the Stoics became important in Greek culture, possibly under the influence of oriental religions encountered during the movements of the troops of Alexander the Great. These Stoics launched a much-needed reform against excesses common to agrarian folk religions. In order to eliminate ritual intoxication and sexually explicit fertility rites, it seemed necessary to remove all passion and deep feelings. Thus they placed emotion of all kinds under suspicion. Because of Neo-Platonism and the strong influences of scholar-theologians such as Augustine, this dichotomy between body and spirit persisted into the Renaissance and the eighteenth-century Enlightenment. In fact, despite the contemporary hue and cry for holistic approaches affirming high emotion, most of middle-class Western society today is far better at discussing emotive celebration than at practicing it.

As a result of this history of more than two thousand years, the word *emotion* itself has suffered from gross misrepresentation. All too often the term seems to connote only the lower emotions: fear, lust, hate, prejudice, and paranoid distrust. We confuse "emotion and emotionalism, defining the quality by its extreme" (Craddock, *Authority*, p. 85). In point of fact, the word denotes the whole spectrum: high and low; good and less than good; intense as well as moderate. So the oft-maligned category of emotion includes the highest goals of all preaching, and every preacher needs to affirm and be at ease expressing godly emotion.

Oddly enough, we have considered it quite acceptable for advertisers and merchants to deal in emotions in the blatant pursuit of commercial gain. Yet we preachers have been supposed to seek the salvation and maturation of precious souls under a mandate that allows only the Holy Spirit to stir the emotions directly, and unaided by any understanding or action on our part. We feel we dare not become involved in such things. Our own feelings are considered to be insufficiently holy for us to touch the emotions of others in the usages of worship. But there is hope; this would seem to be the sort of "demon" that, when it can be named, can be cast out.

We can't dance freely like David and the Ethiopian debtura, but knowing the nature of these undercurrents, we could become more spontaneous. It may not be easy to switch our intuitive responses and those of our audiences to freely expressive celebration. It will require very slow and purposeful effort to accomplish the change of cultural biases and expectations, but it can be done. We call such changes "acculturation."

To start this process we must understand that emotions control so much of a whole person's experience that psychiatrists devote more time to emotion than to anything else. In this significant new awareness many thoughtful people today are at least theoretically committed to the *idea* that we should no longer be ashamed of our emotions. Grown men are now advised to cry in public and cease repressing their deep feelings. Many learned clergy have even come to appreciate when they can report that after the sermon there was hardly a dry eye in the house. Of course they don't want to gain a reputation for being "tear-jerkers," like many star television preachers. But emotion is much too essential for us to cede it exclusively to the counterfeiters.

It should come as no surprise that one can find help toward the removal of inhibitions from psychiatrists and others in the healing arts. It was they who alerted us to the perils of dualism, and they have long urged a holism that would permit joyous dance and song. What they have advised about getting in touch with one's emotions is readily accomplished in the accepting, permissive environment of a worshiping family of God. That is, if and when one can slowly acculturate them to openness of mind and spirit on the matter.

Thus, to remove inhibitions, we have to become intentional about emotion in worship as a whole. We have always spoken against lukewarm or cold worship, even though we have not worked sufficiently hard to grasp what *warm* worship might be like. Preaching, as the key element in Protestant worship, has been all along under the obligation to be warm, or emotionally moving. But we have not faced squarely the emotional character of faith and hope and love. So it is not hard to see why we haven't figured out how to communicate with and feed emotional entities. It is time to deal with the nurture of faith by means of warm and intentionally emotive sharing of the gospel, concluding with sound and spontaneous emotional expressions called "celebration."

The powerful effects of emotion must begin to be systematically utilized, rather than merely tolerated. This is mandated if faith at the level of core belief and practice is to grow. Just as muscles must be exercised to develop physically, so must feelings. For this precise purpose, worship must now be planned as well as preparation for preaching. A congregation sings, "O for a thousand tongues to sing my great Redeemer's praise," and the emotive joy of singing nurtures praise and faith in the process. They sing, "It is well with my soul," and this emotionally moving affirmation strengthens their tapes of trust. It is etched, as it were, on "fleshy tablets" of the soul, which sings it wholeheartedly through the involvement of the voice and the whole person that goes with it. The effect is neither mechanical nor final, but it has significant influence, as empowered by the Holy Spirit. Just as we have chosen moving hymns, so must we choose elements in preaching that exercise high emotions like faith, trust, love, and hope.

The celebration techniques suggested in chapter 3 are essential to *every* sermon, and so important for just this reason; they are not mere cultural distinctives of a particular ethnic group. It is universally true that people recall far better what they have celebrated well; and they are far more apt to grow in Christian behavior—areas about which they have authentically rejoiced. Frank Thomas says bluntly, "They will neither remember nor practice what they have not celebrated." Some may deal with emotion irresponsibly and unethically, but it must be dealt with in *some* way by *all* who would preach for the holistic growth of persons.

This is far from anti-intellectual. Educational research has confirmed the idea that what we celebrate (get emotional about) we retain far longer. Educators have joined the healers in affirming that celebration provides what I have mentioned as the "ecstatic reinforcement" of the lesson or content offered in the sermon. George Leonard, former editor of *Look* magazine, reported in his book *Education and Ecstasy* that children read best and remembered most the things about which the teachers helped them to be glad. Celebration is therefore to be sought, among many other reasons, for the way in which it can lift up the "meat" of the message and render it unforgettable.

But intellectual recall is not all. There is a sense in which the depths of human intuition are closely related to the emotions, which causes the joy to affect values and levels of trust. High commitment and deep trust are far more likely to develop in an emotionally charged atmosphere. The joyous singing of the Civil Rights era, like earlier songs in labor unions and army contingents, became the very backbone of the mass movement. And many a television news report of even the Chinese uprisings and the movements against the Iron Curtain showed hundreds of thousands united and empowered by emotionally sung and shouted slogans. There is that much strength in commitment, which, when holistic, involves intuition and emotion as well as logic.

Western Christianity has begun to give lip service to this holistic ideal of celebration. Biblical scholars of varying positions seem to agree that the dualism apparent in passages like Paul's lament in Romans (7:24) is not real. Paul's own more Hebraic ideas, then, were colored by the use of his family's second language and culture. The surface reading of Paul, combined with the association of emotion with the supposedly evil flesh, has had a lot to do with the inability of many to take seriously our first biblical injunction to "rejoice before the Lord." But that is changing.

The ultimate price for failing to nurture authentic celebration is that joy inhibited in expression is joy diminished or outright lost. The manners in which it is expressed may vary greatly; all "shouting" is not equally audible. But genuine joy does not exist without some form of release or expression. Blessings lifted up in praise are blessings enjoyed or celebrated on an unlimited rerun basis, to use the summer television figure. The tragic alternatives are either that the sermon without a celebration is without some portion of the Word worthy of such. Or, the inhibition toward deserved celebration and rejoicing causes the material preached to lose its greatest possible effect within the total person.

One place to initiate the process of acculturation is in areas where we already accept celebration: poetry, music, and drama. A flat reading of a poem would be readily rejected. It must be read dramatically throughout, and it must rise to a kind of climactic utterance at the end. A cantata, like a symphony, is required to increase in intensity as it approaches the grand finale. The audience intuitively awaits the crescendo, when the theme is finally restated and lifted to its highest expression. In religious drama, the same sequence would apply, with the expectation revolving around the resolution of the conflict. Again, following the rules of art, the dramatic intensity reaches its zenith and the play draws to an exciting and satisfying conclusion. No art form is allowed simply to dribble to the end or peter out. So also in sermons.

Whole liturgies need to be reconsidered in artistic terms, and this applies especially to the sermon. Although no one should overload the preaching role and expect it to generate miracles, it is a fact that the sermon is the facet of worship over which the minister has the greatest and most direct control. And the acceptability of celebration is more likely to be won here than anywhere else, albeit subtly and by no means in confrontation. It is not an overstatement to say that artistry will win its own acceptance in the intuitive depths of the worshiper, after the rationale has been accepted and a process of intentional emotion has been implemented with sensitivity.

A hearty minority of creative modern Christians has already taken up the challenge. Some have choreographed interpretive dance programs as acts of worship. Others seek to express themselves more freely than standard culture by using instruments such as guitars. One must applaud their commitment, yet most of those who join in the applause find it hard to worship authentically in these new and unavoidably alien modes. It takes a long time to acculturate away from deeply entrenched patterns of worship. And a wise and intentional process, involving all of any congregation, will be required to move peacefully into the growth now so obviously needed in connection with emotions and worship.

WORKING UNDERSTANDINGS CONCERNING EMOTION

As one launches into what is for some a strange new world of intentional emotive expression, the excesses once assumed universal must somehow be ruled out and guaranteed against. Since there may have been no cultural expectations or other restraints in place, one needs what might be called working understandings with which to begin. In some respects it might be called a code of professional ethics. Whatever the name, one needs the security of established patterns of practice as protection against error. One also needs the respect of the constituency, which goes with the observance of an emerging canon of rules and regulations. As one born and reared in a more expressive culture than that of the American majority, I find it not difficult to propose such a set of understandings, since they have been at work in my world all my life.

Our first understanding is to practice an irrevocable commitment to high purpose and to the use of appeals directed to the highest emotions. Evoking tears must never be an end in itself or a means of manipulating monetary gifts, not even for supporting a world hunger project. Patronizing pity, so common earlier in the twentieth century among programs directed to the so-called heathen, is far less than truly Christian, and sinfully smug besides. Powerful emotional impact should be viewed in the same way one views dynamite. It can be most destructive when not used for the purposes for which it was made. The construction of roads and dams is impossible without dynamite. Likewise, the appeal to high emotion is required in the softening of the low emotion of stony pride. So it is also with the commitment of persons to forgiveness or unity or hard work for world peace.

Furthermore, emotional needs can be met only by means involving those same emotions. The discouragement of low emotions, the development of love and other high emotions, the commitment of the will of persons to the will of God, and the healing of hearers in need of emotional and spiritual health—all these demand that sermons have *emotional* impact harnessed to these high purposes.

Once this is settled, we should be freed up to be spontaneous and receive and use our full potential under the Holy Spirit. James A. Forbes offers a word of advice in this connection: "Rather than getting bogged down over specific manifestations [of emotional expressiveness], we should focus on how we can be empowered as a result of receiving the Spirit" (*The Holy Spirit and Preaching*, p. 94). The greatest healings and empowerment often come with the least predictable expressions.

Second, we are obliged to avoid a message unless we feel deeply about the subject. If the preacher does not care *greatly* about the text and its meaning for the hearers, then why should they? The audience takes its subtle but powerful cues from the preacher. False or insincere facsimiles of emotion on the part of the preacher may deceive some, but they never have real spiritual depth and effect. The spoken word has power to move persons often only to the extent that it has already moved the speaker.

Related to this second understanding is a third: the fact that emotion travels between the members of a warm and caring fellowship by *contagion*. This is surely not a fresh revelation to anyone who has ever attended a Christian funeral. The same is true of the touching movie in which rank strangers are moved together by a common identification with the film's characters. The hymn speaks truthfully about some of our experiences when it says, "We share our mutual woes." The power of this contagion is perhaps best validated when persons who are determined not to cry with the majority of an audience are utterly defeated. This offers sweeping challenges to the discipline of sermon preparation and to the integrity of the preacher in the uses made of this inevitable contagion.

Reading it another way, there is a sense in which the Holy Spirit has allies in the congregation. The more outwardly spontaneous persons help those who are more subtly inhibited, influencing them by empathy, identification, and contagion, within limits. This tends to free the latter to manifest more feeling, thus enhancing their own experience of the Word. This does not necessarily imply histrionic outbursts; an atmosphere may be emotionally charged with no obvious sounds or easily visible expressions. The preacher ought not to work at eliciting overt evidence of in-depth response. The spiritual and emotional quality of the preacher and the liberated hearers will communicate without crass, manipulative cues and the clamor of claques.

Within the cultural expectations of any community of worshipers, the Holy Spirit is, after all, the primary "mover and shaker." Whatever the apparent dynamics, the Holy Spirit has so fixed it that there can never be human predictions of authentic results, nor may human beings ever take credit. Efforts at authentic reruns of the work of the Spirit are doomed to failure. Jesus suggested that the Spirit was like unpredictable winds in the prescientific eras.

Fourth, ponder the threatening fact that emotional considerations must be a part of sermon preparations from the very *outset*. Knowing that emotion is inescapable, the preacher must weigh each homiletical move for impact or effect. The preacher needs, as far as possible, to make sure that the emotional involvement and suspense ascend progressively, to the final celebration. Preachers themselves are the measuring rods.

This concluding element is the essential ecstatic reinforcement of the Word for all people. There is more on this subject in chapter 3, on outlines. Suffice it to say that this sort of planned timing of impact is not to be mistaken for what is pejoratively referred to as "manipulation." This is high art, as well as universal emotional logic.

Just as a dramatist writes a play whose acts move up to the resolution of the conflict, and just as a composer creates a symphony whose movements climb to the last crescendo, a sermon lifts up and finally celebrates its good news. The logic of emotive consciousness is as important and coherent as the logic of human reason. Human emotion instinctively requires that the impact escalate, and assumes closure when peak and downturn are signaled. All beyond this is anticlimactic, losing attention automatically.

The logic of reason is not to be ignored because of this; the two logics must be synthesized in order to provide experiential encounter for the whole person. The Holy Spirit can be counted on to use this more insightful and disciplined preparation to create and nurture new persons in Christ. This has always been the case with the most powerful preachers of all cultures and schools of theology.

Finally, the preacher needs *carefully* to select vivid details. Oftentimes it is the details that determine how deeply involved the hearer will be in the experiential encounter. The associations called forth may be emotionally cathartic and healing of pain; there may be feelings of righteous indignation; or they may be joyous, irrepressible waves of praise and celebration. Whatever the character of the response, deep emotions are moved to expression by identification with familiar specifics of place, problem, or other details.

The very word *identification* literally denotes emotional bonding. However much the details may seem intellectually unimportant, they gain their spiritual impact primarily from the way they move the hearer toward *feelings* of bonding. This is with protagonists, problems, and potentials, to the end of growth for the hearer toward newness in Christ.

The sermon and the worship environment encourage the hearer to express feeling when it is in a permissive and supportive setting. The vital connection between the hearer and the movement in the sermon is a matter of feeling-with, provided that the word has passed the entrance tests of coherence. This greatly healing and liberating experience acquires ecstatic, celebrative dimensions, which reinforce the encounter. This occurs in large part because of the self-recognition and identification borne of the careful selection of descriptive details.

One easily senses how this process worked in a Women's Day sermon at a church in California. The assigned biblical theme came from Luke 8:43-48, and concerned the woman with the issue of blood. Ella P. Mitchell, the preacher, told the story in carefully expanded detail. She used modern medical terms to describe the various diagnoses offered by the series of physicians to whom the woman had paid her life savings. The largely female audience identified with and "came aboard," each as her own malady was mentioned. Or they related to one of the diagnoses in someone dear to them. The effect was awesome. The message of healing faith was planted deep, beyond all forgetting, by using emotional identification with this hemorrhaging woman who dared to touch the hem of Jesus' garment.

Access to emotive consciousness may be gained powerfully and unashamedly through well-timed and carefully chosen configurations of detail, both biblical and nonbiblical. This is altogether fitting and proper, since Jesus himself did it so well and often; and also because it is employed in the lofty and challenging task of being used by God to generate deep emotional and spiritual growth. People need desperately to grow up unto Christ in all sectors of consciousness (Eph. 4:15), and the emotive is often the key to both retention and commitment.

It is quite common to hear conversations about how psychiatry is used to heal *emotional* disorders, yet too often we preach to every sector save that one. To opt to deal with fewer than all the sectors of human consciousness is to fail willfully to deal with the whole person. To struggle to overcome cultural biases against the emotive, and to help others to do so, may well become the most rewarding enterprise of an entire career.

In the chapters that precede, the details mentioned are employed in the various literary genres and in proper sequence, to achieve the high purpose of new creatures in Christ, growing up to him in all aspects of human personality. This is enhanced by means of identification, encounter, and celebration. May it be so for seminary students as they minister, and for all God's servants who engage in the labor of reading and practicing the insights offered here.

A SELECTED
BIBLIOGRAPHY

Achtemeier, Elizabeth. *Creative Preaching*. Nashville: Abingdon Press, 1980.

Berne, Eric. *Intuition and Ego States*. New York: Harper & Row, 1977.

Buttrick, David G. *Homiletic: Moves and Structures*. Philadelphia: Fortress Press, 1987.

_____. *Preaching Jesus Christ; An Exercise in Homiletic Theology*. Philadelphia: Fortress Press, 1988.

_____. *A Captive Voice: The Liberation of Preaching*. Louisville: Westminster John Knox Press, 1994.

Buttrick, George A. *The Parables of Jesus*. Garden City, N.Y.: Doubleday, Doran, 1928; Grand Rapids, Mich.: Baker Book House, 1973.

Cannon, Katie G. *Teaching Preaching*. New York: Continuum, 2002.

Cox, James W. *Preaching*. San Francisco: Harper & Row, 1985.

Craddock, Fred B. *As One Without Authority: Essays on Inductive Preaching*. Enid, Okla.: Phillips University Press, 1971; St. Louis: Chalice Press, 2001.

_____. *Overhearing the Gospel*. Nashville: Abingdon Press, 1978.

_____. *Preaching*. Nashville: Abingdon Press, 1985.

Davis, H. Grady. *Design for Preaching*. Philadelphia: Fortress Press, 1958.

Eslinger, Richard L. *A New Hearing*. Nashville: Abingdon Press, 1987.

Forbes, James A., Jr. *The Holy Spirit and Preaching*. Nashville: Abingdon Press, 1989.

Jensen, R. A. *Telling the Story*. Minneapolis: Augsburg Press, 1980.

LaRue, Cleophus J. *The Heart of Black Preaching*. Louisville: Westminster John Knox Press, 2000.

Leonard, George B. *Education and Ecstasy*. New York: Delacorte Press, 1968.

Lowry, Eugene L. *The Homiletical Plot: The Sermon as Narrative Art Form*. Atlanta: Westminster John Knox Press, 1980, 2001.

_____. *Doing Time in the Pulpit: The Relationship between Narrative and Preaching*. Nashville: Abingdon Press, 1985.

_____. *How to Preach a Parable: Designs for Narrative Sermons*. Nashville: Abingdon Press, 1989.

Lundblad, Barbara K. *Transforming the Stone*. Nashville: Abingdon Press, 2001.

Markquart, Edward F. *Quest for Better Preaching*. Minneapolis: Augsburg Press, 1985.

Massey, James E. *Designing the Sermon*. Nashville: Abingdon Press, 1980.

Mitchell, Henry H. *Black Preaching*. Philadelphia: J. B. Lippincott, 1970; New York: Harper & Row, 1979; Nashville: Abingdon Press, 1990.

_____. *The Recovery of Preaching*. New York: Harper & Row, 1977.

_____. *Celebration and Experience in Preaching*. Nashville: Abingdon Press, 1990.

Pannenberg, Wolfhart. "Focal Essay: The Revelation of God in Jesus of Nazareth," in *Theology as History*, James M. Robinson and John B. Cobb, eds. New York: Harper & Row, 1967.

_____. "Faith and Reason." in *Basic Questions in Theology*. Vol. 2. Philadelphia: Fortress Press, 1971.

_____. *The Apostles' Creed in the Light of Today's Questions*. Philadelphia: Westminster Press, 1972.

Peck, M. Scott. *People of the Lie*. New York: Simon & Schuster, 1983.

Rice, Charles L. *The Embodied Word: Preaching as Art and Liturgy*. Minneapolis: Fortress Press, 1991.

_____. *Interpretation and Imagination: The Preacher and Contemporary Literature.* Philadelphia: Fortress Press, 1970.

Ricoeur, Paul. "Paul Ricoeur on Biblical Hermeneutics," in *Semeia* 4, ed. John Dominic Crossan. Society of Biblical Literature, 1975.

Smith, Robert, Jr. *Doctrine That Dances.* Nashville: B & H Publishing Group, 2008.

TeSelle, Sallie McFague. *Speaking in Parables.* Philadelphia: Fortress Press, 1975.

Thomas, Frank A. *They Like To Never Quit Praisin' God: The Role of Celebration in Preaching.* Cleveland: Pilgrim Press, 1997.

Watson, J. V. "Two Sermons by Brother Carper: The Eloquent Negro Preacher," in *Tales and Takings, Sketches and Incidents, from the Itinerant Budget of Rev. J. V. Watson, Editor of the Northwestern Christian Advocate.* New York, 1856. Quoted by Russell Ritchie and H. Dean Trulear in *American Baptist Quarterly*, vol. 71, no. 1 (March 1987).

Wilson, Paul Scott. *The Practice of Preaching.* Nashville: Abingdon Press, 1995.

INDEX